CONCILIUM

8.95

concilium 1994/3

ISLAM: A CHALLENGE FOR CHRISTIANITY

Edited by

Hans Küng and
Jürgen Moltmann

SCM Press · London
Orbis Books · Maryknoll

Published by SCM Press Ltd, 26–30 Tottenham Road, London N1
and by Orbis Books, Maryknoll, NY 10545

ISBN: 0 334 03026 9 (UK)
ISBN: 0 88344 878 5 (USA)

Typeset at The Spartan Press Ltd, Lymington, Hants
Printed by Mackays of Chatham, Kent

Concilium Published February, April, June, August, October, December.

20023368

297

Contents

Editorial: Islam – A Challenge to Christianity

The wars of olden times were wars between kings and princes; those of the nineteenth and twentieth centuries were wars of nations and ideologies. The wars of the twentieth century will be wars of civilizations. That, at any rate, is the thesis of the Harvard professor Samuel Huntington, put forward in the summer 1993 edition of the journal *Foreign Affairs*. That Islam could emerge as an aggressor in such a 'clash of civilizations' is the fear of many people in the West and perhaps the hope of some Muslim fundamentalists and radicals. And we have to grant that certainly in our days there is no lack of tensions and aggressions, not only on the part of Islam but also on the part of some 'Christian' countries (one need only look at Bosnia-Herzegovina).

But the thesis of the threat of a 'clash of civilizations' is only a half-truth. For the civilizations and religions have not only a high potential for conflict but also a high potential for peace, which they have shown not only in the revolution in Eastern Europe but also in the removal of the dictatorship in the Philippines and the abolition of Apartheid in South Africa. A war between the civilizations and even between the religions is in no way something which has to be accepted fatalistically, above all not if the potential of the religions for peace and reconciliation can be a ferment in particular civilizations.

That is the starting point of this issue. It aims to bring Christianity and Islam together – for all the insuperable differences between them – in a spirit of peace. For we begin with one basic conviction. Of course Islam represents a challenge to Christianity, just as Christianity represents a challenge to Islam. But a challenge need not become a threat, far less violent aggression. So in this issue we have been concerned to maintain the style of a dialogue. Central points of controversy like monotheism, human rights and views of history are treated from both Muslim and Christian perspectives, so that readers can consider standpoints from the eyes of those of another faith. Anyone who reads the issue carefully will have the important experience that just as Christianity appears in many forms, so too today there are various forms of Islam. Any monolithic approach leads to fatal generalizations and is not worthy of an ecumenical theology.

Ecumenical theology came into being as it became possible to get beyond thinking of differences within Christianity in terms of friend and foe, and in turn is passionately opposed to constructing new hostile images, whether in Christianity against Islam or in Islam against the 'Western Satan'. After the loss of the Communist 'enemy', some apocalyptists in religion and politics evidently need new 'enemies' to justify their aggressive identity and unite and dominate their own society. But anyone who seeks the 'clash of civilizations' or even 'the mother of all battles' does not serve life but death. Ecumenical theology is the theology of a shared life and a theology of peace.

Hans Küng's concluding article on 'World Peace – World Religions – World Ethic' is his farewell to the *Concilium* section on Ecumenism. For thirty years, since 1965, he has directed this section, first alone, then with Walter Kasper, and finally with Jürgen Moltmann. However, Hans Küng will remain committed to the work of *Concilium*. As a founder of the journal he will remain a member of the Editorial Committee of *Concilium* – as long as he so wishes – and thus will continue to support the concern of this journal and help to direct its course. Jürgen Moltmann will continue his work as director of the section for a while yet. From the next number Hans Küng's place will be taken by the Tübingen Catholic theologian and ecumenist Karl-Josef Kuschel. As a pupil of Hans Küng he will continue the work of ecumenism both inside and outside the churches.

Jürgen Moltmann
Hans Küng

I · Experiences

Bosnia: The Challenge of a Tolerant Islam

Smail Balić

The further holocaust which to the world's dismay is taking place in Europe at the end of the twentieth century has brought into the spotlight of international publicity a peripheral Islam, that of the Bosniacs or Bosnians in the national sense.

The continuing history of this Islam goes back to the encounter of the Bosnians with the military power of the Osmans in the fifteenth century. It was preceded by an Islamic presence in parts of the Hungarian empire, predominantly in Srijem, north-east Bosnia and north-west Serbia, which was interrupted by force. This lasted from the beginning of the eighth century to the end of the thirteenth. For more than half a millennium the original population of Bosnia observed the Islam of a relatively liberal Hanafitic school of interpretation.

Initially, Bosnian Islam had a markedly mystical character and in addition displayed some Gnostic features. This was expressed in the character of its teachers, mystics and pioneers who with their religious view of the world contributed a number of syncretistic elements. On the whole religious exclusiveness was alien to them. They understood themselves as seekers of the divine truth (*sālikūn fī sabīlillāh*). Muhammad was accepted by the Bosnians only as a saint – a new saint in the long line of already existing saints. Today the simple Bosnian Muslim still swears 'Sveca mi moga Muhameda' ('By my saint, Muhammad!'). Like the Bektashi mystics, the spiritual guardians of the Janissaries, the Bosnian Muslims tend to be somewhat lax in their religious practice. Their popular poetry shows them to be people open to the world, cheerful and not disinclined to enjoy wine. Links with Christian and Jewish neighbours, initially above all through the female line, were quite frequent among them. In this century, in the cities up to ten per cent of marriages were mixed, and in individual cases Muslim women also had Christian partners.

The Muslims did not arrive in Bosnia in the fifteenth and sixteenth centuries, as some parties tendentiously claim. They are the old indigenous element there. Before they became Muslims they were predominantly members of a Protestant-style Christian sect which scholars know under the name of Patarenes. It was related to the French Cathari and Albigensians. Its picture of Christ was virtually Arian. Christ was regarded as God's foremost creature, predominantly as Spirit (*rūḥ*). This gave the sect an affinity to Islam, and there was a series of other common doctrines.

Patarenism, incorrectly called Bogomilism, which was bitterly persecuted by the two great churches, saw the Osman thrust northwards as a chance of rescuing at least some of its essence. Hitherto the Paterenes had seen themselves largely also as the guardians of Bosnian state and cultural independence. The common interest in both directions – state and religion – led to an alliance. In the fifteenth and sixteenth centuries the supporters of the 'Bosnian church', another name for the Bosnian heresy, along with other Bosnians, went over to Islam more or less *en masse*. From then on they played a prominent role in the Osman empire as politicians (viziers and pashas), soldiers and clergy. Their homeland, Bosnia, which must be seen as including Herzegovina as its southern part, named after a local count, enjoyed a large degree of autonomy until 1831, when the short-lived independent 'Bosnian Eyālet' was destroyed by the Sultan's troops.

With the Austro-Hungarian occupation of their land in 1878, the Bosnians and thus also the Muslims came into close contact with Western European culture. Since then a powerful process of Europeanization has taken place among them. Even religious thought was quite considerably affected by this. The most important reformers were Muhamed Nasih Pajić (died 1918), Mehmed Džemaludin Čaušević (died 1938) and Osman Nuri Hadžić (died 1939).[1]

There is much reflection and criticism in Bosnian Islam. As an illustration here are two examples from the Islamic publicity still used in the last phase of Communist rule in ex-Yugoslavia. A college-trained Imam, Zijad Ljevaković, expresses his discontent over the tendencies towards 'an Islamicization of science' and writes: 'There are books like *Medicine in the Qur'an*, *Psychology in the Qur'an* and the like. They are appearing at a time when the whole Islamic world is treating itself with medications of Western origin. When illnesses develop, people seem to prefer to go to non-Muslim hospitals. The whole of medical practice is build up on foreign medical systems. People constantly say that everything is already in the Qur'an. But no one is in a position to put into practice what is supposed to be there. To claim that something that has only been discovered in Europe with much toil and trouble is unfair and bears witness to a strange blindness.'[2]

Here is another voice which is sharply critical of circumstances in the Islamic world (the author is the Bosnian journalist Amir Sehić): 'When I compare Muhammad's success with the failure of today's preachers of Islam, it becomes clear to me where the difference between them lies. I involuntarily think of the Qur'anic statement (4.113) that in addition to revelation, Muhammad was also endowed with wisdom and knowledge. What we need today in order to find our place in the world and act in accordance with the new situation which has arisen are precisely wisdom and a knowledge of things.'[3]

I. The role of Islam in the conflict between Bosnians and Serbs

Bosnian Islam in no way contributed to the setting of the bloody scene in Bosnia in 1992/93. If there is any mention of its role in this context, it can only be of a fate which it drew upon itself. The Muslims in ex-Yugoslavia are simply 'guilty' of existing. In the lamentable genocide they are the objects of the vengeance of Serbian extremists and a large part of the Serbian Orthodox church for the supposed faults and misdeeds of their ancient ancestors.

The real motive for Serbian aggression against Bosnia lies in a greed for power and an effort to erect a greater Serbian state on the ruins of Yugoslavia. The motive power which to a high degree manipulates the Serbian masses is a 'historical memory' supported by the myth of a heavenly vocation of the Serbian people. The Serbian drive towards an old-fashioned kind of heroism which is incapable of any true humanity can be misused as a welcome mechanism for mobilization. The translation of such a heroic ideal into practice produces devastating results in a highly industrialized age. As the destruction and forms of holocaust in Bosnia show, this combination of antiquity and highly developed military techniques is as catastrophic as it is monstrous. This last characteristic of the genocide in Bosnia is all the more terrifying, since those involved in the drama observe no ethical norms.

Serbian Orthodoxy, an important motive force in these events, draws on retarded theological thought; it is fixated on history and backed up by an evidently militaristic spirit. But paradoxically Islam in the Balkans has long since given up its militant character: the Muslims in ex-Yugoslavia were honest supporters of the 'brotherhood and unity' solution imposed by

Tito and his colleagues. To their disaster they believed that this notion would be preserved for ever. They did not take seriously all the inflammatory propaganda which was quite openly launched against them by the mass media in Belgrade. They attributed the occasional profanations of mosques before the outbreak of the conflict (for example in Trebinje, Bijeljina and Belgrade) and murders – thirty Muslims were murdered in Bosnia alone before the beginning of the hostilities proper – to isolated fanatics. But behind these attacks there was a deeply-rooted anti-Islamic mood among wide circles of the Serbian population. In their eyes the move over to Islam had been treachery to the nation.

Islam is presented by official Serbian propaganda as an originally fundamentalist and thus militant religion. Consequently expansionist aims are attributed to the Muslim Bosnians. As these propagandists say, a 'green transverse line' connects them through the Sanjak of Novi Pazar and the Battle of Kosovo or the Wardar valley with Adrianople and Istanbul, thus providing a direct link with the rest of the Islamic world. It is claimed that they wanted to found an 'Islamic republic', although this goes against the religious restraint in Bosnian political thought. In reality the Bosnian Muslims are largely secularized, open to the world, tolerant and orientated on the West.

Talk of 'treachery' as the result of a change of faith is, however, an anachronism in the twentieth century. It builds on notions which have been left behind. For consistency, Protestant Christianity too would have traitors as members. On the other hand the Bosnians are not Serbs at all, so they can hardly be accused of treachery through apostasy from a supposed Orthodoxy which in fact they rejected.

On the hypothesis that the Serbian interpretation of the process of Islamicization in Bosnia could have some real basis, Alois Schmaus, the German translator of the anti-Islamic poem *Gorski vijenac* (The Mountain Garland) by the Montenegran bishop Petar Petrović Njegoš (died 1851), asks himself: 'If the move to Islam made out of opportunism and self-advantage [as claimed by Serbian historiography] can be imputed to the first generation as treachery and sin, can later generations be made responsible for it? Is not extremely un-Christian and a blatant injustice to make women and children do penance for the deeds of distant ancestors?'

The coupling of Islam with Turkish rule and a historical view of Bosnia and its people have left their stamp on the attitude of the Serbian church and helped it to develop into one of the most dangerous destructive forces in the Balkans. This attitude, which has found literary expression and a quasi-scientific basis in the works of fanatics like Miroslav Jevtić and Vojislav Šešelj, was described by Alois Schmaus – as much later by Jevtić himself, like this: 'By retaining an awareness of historical connections and constantly renewing for themselves the decisions made then, by emphasizing the victory of the Turks at Kosovo and deriving their rights to rule from that, they have a share in the original sin of the nation and in each generation and each individual renew the one-time betrayal of the legacy of their ancestors. Conversely the Christian Montenegrans constantly renew their decision along the lines of Obilić: they remain loyal to the legacy and feel it an obligation down to the time of Danilo [a predecessor of Bishop Njegoš].'

The Greater Serbian national spirit with its religious gloss needs special examination in terms of the psychology of peoples. Many changes in reality underlie the world-view of those who are stamped by this spirit. They are often irrational in their behaviour and actions. Popular singers turned a defeat like that which took place in 1389 at Kosovo into an exaggerated event of national greatness. The national epic links up with this. In the eyes of the people, Mrnjacević Marko, the vassal of the Turks, became the great popular hero Kraljević Marko. In the intoxication of freedom at the beginning of the nineteenth century and in the period of nationalistic Romanticism their Muslim neighbours were suddenly seen as arch-enemies, although the Serbs had derived some advantage from the shadow of these neighbours during the Osman period as merchants, cavalry (Spahis), Martolosen and Vojnukān (two types of troops made up of Christians) – as watchmen (*derbentjis*), interpreters and spies.

The actions of the Bosnian Muslims, some of which had been to the advantage of the Serbians, like the opening up of the Hungarian settlement to Serbian traders, the restoration of the Serbian patriarchate of Peć by Mehmed Pasaha Sololović and the settling of the Serbs in central and western Bosnia and in Croatia, were forgotten. It has also completely escaped the Croats that it was only as a result of the policy of the Grand Vizier Ahmed Pasha Hercegović-Hrsekzāde that the republic of Ragusa (Dubrovnik) was left out of the Osman plans for conquest and remained alive. Today the two neighbouring extreme nationalisms are working on the extermination of Bosnianism and its Islam.

II. Fruitless attempts at dialogue with the Serbian Orthodox church

The Re:īs ul-ʿulemāʾ, the supreme head of the Islamic community, has made repeated efforts to meet the patriarch. However, the first concrete possibility for such a meeting was destroyed by the war situation in Sarajevo. There was to have been a meeting of all three religious leaders in

Geneva on 23 September 1992 at the invitation of the World Council of Churches. However, only Cardinal Kuharić and Patriarch Pavle came. The Re-ī ul-ʿulemā', Jakub Efendi Selimoski, could only fax through his prepared speech. Some of it describes the situation of Islam in the Bosnian conflict:

> The whole republic is like its capital Sarajevo: it is utterly in flames and ruins, deafened by explosions and in a sea of human blood. All that had hitherto been built up over centuries with the great effort and sacrifices of many generations lies in dust and ashes. Bosnia is now torn apart by a violence and a hatred which are incomprehensible.
>
> Until yesterday this land was a model of harmony, tolerance and multicultural life and custom. In Sarajevo, the Gazi Husrewbeg mosque, the Orthodox church, the Catholic cathedral and the Jewish synagogue stood quite close together. For centuries they served their faithful without one group ever getting in the way of another. Rather, they supplemented one another in harmony.
>
> As servants of religion we do not have the task of engaging in politics. But we think that it is legitimate to ask the question, Where is this unspeakable hatred coming from? What is the source of these base impulses towards annihilation, the source of blood, of these atrocities unparalleled in history? What is the source of something like this among members of a nation which confesses the gospel of peace – a message which communicates a whole scale of true values on which moreover European civilization has been built up?
>
> When we raised our voices in warning before the war over a number of attacks on our religious objects, we also stressed that our modern history knows of no Muslim attack on religious objects of another religion or confession. We asked why this was done to us. At the same time we called on our faithful to show peace, dignity and tolerance.
>
> We are well aware that there are tares in any wheat, so we hoped that the evil came from a small number of extremists, from those who love neither God nor man and who do not observe the word of the gospel. And we asked both the church and the state authorities to do something to stop this development. Since then, after these five months of war, we note with the deepest pain that around 500 mosques have been completely or partially destroyed and burned down. That is the situation as we can assess it on the basis of the data at our disposal. But this alone shows quite clearly that the lamentable barbarism has far surpassed the degree of inhumanity at the time of the blackest Fascism.[4]

In the meantime much more damage has been done in Bosnia than is complained of in the document above. So far the patriarch and the church have not had the courage to condemn the evil in all its concrete forms. Rather, one has the feeling that the Serbian Orthodox church has made itself an important accomplice of the criminal regime in Serbia.

This feeling was further reinforced by remarks made by the patriarch during his visits to Germany and Austria in November 1993. Far be it from the author of this article to offend the patriarch: I personally have respect for the old man. But he is simply standing things on their head. Thus he claims that the Bosnian Muslims came into the country with the Turks. But the opposite is the case: most of the Bosnian Serbs were brought into the country by the Turks. Politicians and the church should have told Pavle the truth in the Federal Republic and in Austria. The whole world knows the aggressor in Bosnia, otherwise there would be no sanctions against the Serbs. In concrete terms, so far Patriarch Pavle has failed. Words are not enough. How right Eugen Rot was in saying, 'There is nothing good unless one does it!'

The portrayal of Bosnian Islam as an allegedly fundamentalist trouble-spot for Europe has recently also become a favourite occupation of Croatian propaganda. This is meant to divert attention from the atrocities of the Croatian-Fascist military in Herzegovina (in Stolac, Čapljina, Počitelj and Mostar) and in Central Bosnia (Kiseljak, Ahmići, Vitez). But any kind of fundamentalist attitude is alien to the average Bosnian Muslim. 'Of course there are also nutcases in Bosnia,' remarks a journalist from Sarajevo, 'who would like to organize their lives towards the creation of an Islamic republic in accordance with religious norms, but in Bosnia everyone is aware that that is impossible, a sheer delusion. The mere attempt to put such ideas into practice would amount to an act of violence against the Bosnian Muslims themselves, because as a European people they have deep roots in the political tradition of the West. They therefore want to maintain unswervingly the European model of political life and civilization.[5] After the passing of the Bosnian Muslim declaration on democracy and Europe, the so-called 'Proclamation of 10 July 1991', no one may have any doubts about that.[6]

Translated by John Bowden

Notes

1. Anyone interested to know more of their work and significance is referred to my book *Das unbekannte Bosnien* (see bibliography below).

2. *Preporod*, the journal of the Islamic community in Bosnia, Sarajevo, 1 March 1991, no. 492, 15.

3. Amir Sehić, 'Interpretacija islama', *Takvim*, Sarajevo 1975, 26.

4. The entire text of this memorandum was published in *Glaube in der 2.Welt* 20, 1992, 11.

5. Esad Hećimović, 'Kako zavaditi Bosanske Muslimane?' ('How could division be sown among Bosnian Muslims?'), *Ljiljan*, Sarajevo and Ljublana, 15 December 1993, 4.

6. Published in German in my *Das unbekannte Bosnien* (see below), 371–3.

For further reading

Rabia Ali and Lawrence Lifschultz (eds.), *Why Bosnia? Writings on the Balkan War*, Stony Creek, Conn. 1993

Abduselam Balagiya, *Les Musulmans yougoslaves. Étude sociologique*, Algiers 1940

Smail Balić, *Das unbekannte Bosnien. Europas Brücke zur islamischen Welt*, Cologne, Weimar and Vienna 1992

Maximilian Braun, *Die Anfänge der Europäisierung in der Literatur der muslimischen Sklaven in Bosnien und Herzegowina*, Leipzig 1934

Robert J. Donia, *Islam under the Double Eagle. The Muslims of Bosnia and Herzegovina. 1878–1914*, New York 1981

Africa: Why Christians are Turning Toward Islam

Patrick D. Gaffney

I. A recovery of the indigenous perspective

The significance of Islam in Africa for Christians may be seen from two perspectives, one global and the other indigenous. Such viewpoints, however, represent a dynamic continuum rather than logical opposites. The principal value of this double approach lies in its acknowledgment of two dimensions, linked by family resemblances, borrowings, overlaps and convergences, in African ways of being Muslim.

Until quite recently, Christian scholars discussing Islam in Africa have tended to concentrate heavily, often exclusively, on authoritative texts, classical institutions and ideological or doctrinal systems with a bias for the idealized expressions of elite Arabic sources. Other manifestations of the faith tended to be ignored or dismissed as heterodox. Often such theologians justified this neglect and superficiality by consigning native practice to a nether world of syncretism: 'In its spread through Tropical Africa . . . Islam became a folk religiion . . . In the process Islam has lost its universalist qualities and assumed the characteristics of a particularist cult, expressing itself in a mélange of localized animistic ritual and Islamic practice which would shock the sensibilities of even the least pious savant.'

Thus one initial motive behind the recent Christian turn toward Islam is to overcome the distortions left by this ethnocentric snobbery so as to encounter the experience of believers. Indeed, one of the signal advances in recent inter-religious dialogue and stressed in the *Lineamenta* for the forthcoming Synod of African Bishops, warns that dialogue should not be approached abstractly as an interface between Islam and Christianity. Rather, it should be carried out as meeting between individuals who are

Muslims or Christians, 'especially when they are members of the same family and tribe or citizens of the same nation'.[2]

But a more substantial stimulus for this Christian turn toward Islam stems from a recovery of the indigenous perspective on their history in the African context. This has occurred in part as a response to uncritical assertions which contend that the diffusion of Christianity in Africa followed as an inextricable strand of colonialism. However, this reduction of the 'missionary factor' to the ideological arm of Western imperialism is supported neither by indigenous testimony nor by the wealth of contrary evidence.[3]

II. Islamization and evangelization in the past

In the first instance, the African heritage claims religious roots that date from the first generation of Christ's apostles as well as the Prophet's companions. Although the far northern littoral was absorbed into the Islamic world by the eighth century, its new conquerors were occupying territory that had for a millennium been incorporated into the Hellenistic imperium in its successive Hellenic, Roman, and Byzantine phases. The replacement of Greek with Arabic as well as conversions from Christianity to Islam proceeded slowly and not always peacefully, emanating outwards from the centres of power. Edging gradually southwards, Islam predominated in the Sahara by the eleventh century and it had penetrated thoroughly into the Sudanic belt by the fourteenth century with the collapse of the Christian kingdoms of Nubia.

By the late fifteenth century, when the Portuguese reacted against the rising hegemony of the Ottomans by setting out to circumnavigate Africa to reach the Indies, Islam had followed the caravan routes into the Sahel of West Africa down to the rim of the Guinean forests. It appears likely that it would have continued its movement across the Niger River and then into the Congo had it not been interrupted by the chain of events that followed from this European mercantile incentive. To this degree, the rival imperial ambitions of Istanbul and Lisbon can be identified as the catalyst for the celebrated 'Scramble for Africa' among the Western European powers that would reach its climax almost four centuries later.

Initially, the quest for wealth, primarily in gold, spices, ivory and slaves, was viewed by Europeans strictly as a maritime endeavour. But as the size and number of the entrepôts increased with the mounting competition, the growing scale of the exploitation caused the destabilizing effects of the coastal trade to be passed ever deeper into the interior. Guns and the staggering rise in the export of slaves for New World plantations drew the

Portuguese into an escalation of conflicts, especially along the Swahili coast on the Indian Ocean, which had the appearance of transplanting the mediaeval antagonism of Christendom and *Dar al-Islam* around the perimeter of Africa.

An awareness of these preliminary European incursions spread along the pilgrimage route connecting Africa to Mecca, heightening the appeal of religiously inspired defensive strategies. In the eighteenth and nineteenth centuries, a wave of reformist movements and *jihads*, typically organized as a militant Sufi confraternity, exploded across the region of present-day Mali, Niger, Burkino Faso, Chad, northern Nigeria and the Sudan, where the last and militarily the most successful of these, the Mahdist state, only fell to an Anglo-Egyptian assault in 1898. By this time, the Berlin Conference that had formalized the carving up of Africa into European 'spheres of influence' had already been over for a decade. The boundaries of protectorates and colonies, later to be independent nations, were already discernible on the map.

But this marked the second, not the first, 'partition' of Africa in modern times. The first had occurred with no fanfare after a series of confrontations between the Portuguese and the Ottomans together with their Arab and African Muslim allies, dividing the continent into three layers. Territories north of a line running roughly between Mogadiscio and Bakar would remain, except for Ethiopia, the preserve of the Sultan. Further south, Christian powers would dominate, while a broad band bisecting the continent just north of the Equator would remain, for the time, contested.

Thus, from an indigenous viewpoint, both Islamization and evangelization are directly tied to a more comprehensive history of imperialist rivalry and domination in Africa. And while the trauma of European colonialization is far more recent than the submersion of the north, with the exception of the passing 'apartheid' implantation of the Boers, it did not supplant native populations and it was incomparably more brief. Nevertheless, the tumultuous acceleration of the pace of change drawing Africa into the twentieth century spared no one. Muslims, Christians and animists alike were all subjected to the inexorable forces of ruthless capitalism, disruptive labour migrations, the decay of the traditional order, the trials of nation building, the demographic explosion, overall impoverishment and colossal culture shock.

III. The recent developments in Christianity and Islam

In responding to these seismic jolts, most Africans who had not yet been exposed to Islam or Christianity were soon absorbed into one community or the other, often enough through the accidents of geography. But in retrospect, it must be noted that the colonial era did not mark the golden age of evangelization, either statistically or in terms of institutional innovation. Nor, indeed, did foreign missionaries necessarily feel that colonial administrators favoured Christianity to the detriment of Islam. For a good number, especially in the early decades, complained that just the opposite was the case. Omitting the initial Portuguese efforts which were disrupted, the beginnings of sustained evangelization in tropical Africa predate the arrival of the colonial regimes by several generations, and at such pioneering centres as Sierra Leone, the Cape Colony and Buganda the foundations of a native church were firmly established well before the flags of England or France were carried inland.

Nevertheless, it is undeniable that the stability and infrastructure development, notably transportation, brought by colonialization enormously quickened the rate of conversions. It is estimated that the continent as a whole advanced from four million Christians in 1900 to close to seven million by 1914. During the same period, Islam increased from sixty million to seventy million adherents. By 1950, on the eve of the transition to national independence, there were approximately thirty million Christians in Africa while the Muslim population had leaped to about four times this number. As I. M. Lewis has noted, the 'total effect of the *pax colonica*, as much involuntarily as intended, was to promote an unprecedented expansion of Islam', such that 'in half a century of European colonization Islam progressed more widely and more profoundly than in ten centuries of precolonial history'.[4]

However, this trend, having the momentum of the past behind it, did not persist beyond the dismantling of the European African empire which was largely complete by the early 1960s. But the churches continued and augmented their rapid growth. By 1975, the number of Christians had soared to almost 100 million. In the early 1990s, it is estimated that this last figure has nearly doubled. Africa is still predominantly Muslim but the balance is shifting steadily towards equity in terms of numbers while the status and influence of the Christian lands, despite their considerable difficulties, is gaining even faster.

IV. Education – inculturation – co-operation in the future

Certainly education counts as one of the key factors in explaining this dizzying transformation, for schooling had sharply contrasting functions in Islamic and Christian communities. Among Muslims, the Qur'an school was usually considered sufficient, for it provided what was needed within a society where the typical pattern of solidarity was a sort of brotherhood or freemasonry which revolved around the authority of a shaykh who not only deliberated on the basis of the *shari'a* or juridical code, as it was understood, but who was also versed in Sufi lore. This combination had proven to be highly adaptive and resilient as it 'inculcated subtle and powerful leadership skills . . . by which all but the most complex or recalcitrant of social situations could be manipulated and reordered'.[5]

But the Africa in which fragile sovereign states were displacing shattered kin and village-based loyalties would require leaders equipped with another form of competence to manage the unfamiliar demands and the confusing opportunities of an uncertain future. The acquisition of literacy which was often held out as a prerequisite for baptism among first generation catechumens became the broad avenue of access to a new and powerful world. Formation in the liberal arts and sciences, however rudimentary, supplied the basic tools for participation in civil society and managing modern technology which represented a quantum leap into a realm beyond the horizon of the tribal elder or the Sufi shaykh. It is in the light of this contrast that the perceptive Jean-Louis Triaud, in commenting on the recent attempts to employ Islam as a strategic tool in African politics, has summarized the outcome by noting that Islam in Africa is 'more manipulated than manipulating'.[6]

Moreover, if the rapid integration of Christianity into African life, aided so substantially by the mission school, has occurred largely in response to the upheaval, estrangement and misery that unleased forces understood in the traditional context as morbid and evil, it is hardly surprising that independent churches arose so frequently in the process. Their stress on mental and physical healing, fertility, exorcism and miraculous/magical protection from danger has often been a vanguard of inculturation, exploring points of convergence between the gospel and the needs of African believers. To this degree, what has appeared to some as the naturalness of Islam's adaptation to the African context has been replicated, perhaps surpassed, by an apparently spontaneous gravitation toward Christianity in so many settings, as Roland Oliver has noted: 'The main lesson of African ecclesiastical history is that the core message tended to run far ahead of its expatriate preachers. Most African societies first received the gospel from fellow Africans. The main contribution of the missionaries was in building the Church.'[7]

Many lessons may be drawn from this sketch that might help advance the dialogue and mutual understanding between Muslims and Christians, but one point stands out in particular. From the indigenous viewpoint, conversions to both religions have reflected efforts to survive, prosper and reinterpret meanings in the face of immediate needs and enduring interests. The present air of competition between Islam and Christianity in Africa which many fear has set them on a 'collision course' may be seen essentially as a continuation, tragic as it is, of a struggle between two extraneous, geopolitical power blocs, masked as the Bible and the Qur'an.[8] But the young church in tropical Africa, in reflecting on its recent experience and the gospel mandate, has every reason to resist being drawn into this mentality. The cry from the heart that 'Muslims and Christians in Africa should be allowed to work out solutions to their problems in their own way rather than being treated as overseas territories by Muslims and Christians elsewhere'[9] may be heard not only as a rejection of yet another 'partition' amounting to a retribalization along religious lines, but it is also an invitation. Africa seems ripe to offer the world an extraordinary example of inter-religious co-operation and interdependence. By basing their dialogue on what unites them, namely all that they have endured and the still greater fears that lie ahead, African Christians and Muslims may give altogether new meaning to the global perspective on this deeply troubled and spiritually essential task of reconciliation.

Notes

1. James Kritzeck and William H. Lewis (eds.), *Islam in Africa*, New York 1969, 7.

2. *The Church in Africa and Her Evangelizing Mission: Towards the Year 2000*, Lineamenta for the Synod of Bishops Special Assembly for Africa, Vatican City 1990, 59. See also Mohamed Talbi, 'Islam and Dialogue – Some Reflections on a Current Topic', in *Christianity Through Non-Christian Eyes*, ed. Paul J. Griffiths, Maryknoll 1990, 82–101.

3. Roland Oliver, *The Missionary Factor in East Africa*, London 1965; Richard Gray, *Black Christians and White Missionaries*, New Haven 1990.

4. I. M. Lewis, *Islam in Tropical Africa*, London 1966, cited in John S. Mbiti, *African Religions and Philosophy*, Nairobi [2]1989, 256; also C. C. Steward, 'Islam', in Andrew Roberts (ed.), *The Colonial Moment in Africa*, Cambridge 1990, 191–222; Lamin Sanneh, 'The Domestication of Islam and Christianity in African Societies', *Journal of Religion in Africa* XI.1, 1980, 1–12.

5. Jay Spaulding, 'An Historical Context for the Study of Islam in Eastern Africa', in Kenneth W. Harrow, *Faces of Islam in African Literature*, Portsmouth, NH 1991, 31.

6. Cited in Catherine Coquery-Vidrovitch, *Africa: Endurance and Change South of the Sahara*, Berkeley 1988, 2.

7. Roland Oliver, *The African Experience*, New York 1991, 204.

8. Olorunfermi John Onaiyekan, 'Christian-Muslim Relations in Africa', *The African Synod*, 3.4, May/June 1992, 9–13.

9. Rabiatu Ammah, 'Muslims and Christians in Africa: The Challenge of Ecumenical Education', in *Theological Education in Africa: Quo Vadimus?*, ed. J. S. Pobee and J. N. Kudadjie, Geneva 1990, 116.

Women in Islam and Christianity.
A Comparison

Riffat Hassan

I. Fundamental assumptions and theological questions

The study of women in the context of any one religious tradition – be it
Islam, Christianity or any other – is a vast and complex enterprise. The
comparison of women in the context of the world's two largest religions –
Islam and Christianity – hardly seems possible given the scope of this
paper. The fact that both 'Islam' and 'Christianity' refer not only to
religious traditions but also to multifarious cultures (encompassed by the
terms 'the world of Islam' and 'the world of Christendom') makes the topic
even broader and more difficult to address in a few pages. Any attempt to
give an over-generalized or simplified overview of the way in which 'Islam'
and 'Christianity' (understood in both their ideal/theoretical and
historical/practical aspects) have perceived women is likely to be too
reductionist in nature to be meaningful. I have chosen, therefore, to
address the multi-faceted and wide-ranging subject in terms of three
foundational assumptions which have had a deep impact on ideas and
attitudes regarding women in the Islamic and Christian traditions.

The belief that men are superior to women characterizes all the major
religions of the world, including Islam and Christianity. In the case of
Christianity and Islam, this belief is rooted in the three foundational
assumptions or myths referred to above. These are: (*a*) that God's
primary creation is man, not woman, since woman is believed to have been
created from man's rib and is therefore derivative and secondary
ontologically; (*b*) that woman, not man, was the primary agent of what is
customarily described as 'Man's Fall' or expulsion from the Garden of
Eden, hence 'all daughters of Eve' are to be regarded with hatred, suspicion
and contempt; and (*c*) that woman was created not only from man but also

for man, which makes her existence merely instrumental and not of fundamental importance.

There are three theological questions to which the above assumptions may appropriately be regarded as answers. These are: 1. How was woman created? 2. Was woman responsible for the 'Fall' of man? 3. Why was woman created? Theoretically speaking, the Islamic and Christian religious traditions differ significantly in the way in which they answer these questions. But practically speaking, both Muslims and Christians have, in general, been patriarchal in their mind-set, creating societies in which men are regarded as the norm and in which woman are considered to be unequal and inferior to men.

It is not possible, within the scope of this article, to deal exhaustively with any of the above-mentioned questions in the context of Islam and/or Christianity. However, an attempt is made in the brief discussion of each question which follows to indicate significant similarities and differences in the way in which the Islamic and Christian traditions, in general, have responded to three foundational assumptions/myths/questions.

II. How was woman created?

The biblical account of the creation of the first human pair consists of two different sources, the Priestly (dated the fifth-century BCE) and the Yahwist (dated the tenth century BCE), from which arise two different traditions which are the subject of an on-going controversy amongst Christian scholars. The belief that woman was made from Adam's rib is rooted in the Yahwist writer's account of creation in Genesis 2.18–24. While Jesus' own attitude to women was positive, and in Mark 10.6 he indicates an affirmation of woman-man equality in creation, the formulators of the Christian tradition, in general, have interpreted the Yahwist account of creation to assert woman's inherent inferiority to man. St Paul is undoubtedly one of the most important formulators of the Christian tradition. His attitude to women has become the subject of heated debate in modern times. Certainly his statements on the issue of man-woman relationship are marked with a certain ambivalence, perhaps even inconsistency. For instance, his use of the Yahwist story of creation to argue woman's subordination to man in I Corinthians 11.3–9 is inconsistent with his message that all believers are equal which is contained in Galatians 3.27–28.

That woman's secondary creation rendered her ontologically inferior and subordinate to man, in accordance with the deutero-Pauline tradition, is heavily stressed in Christian patristic writings and in the first seven ecumenical councils. Of particular significance is the negative impact on women of the writings of *Augustine* and *Aquinas* who were influenced by Paul as well as by the dualistic, androcentric ideas found in Greek-Hellenistic sources. The idea that women were made from 'a bent rib' with 'many carnal abominations' was used by misogynist Inquisitors to condemn 50,000 women as witches and sentence them to death in the period between the fifteenth and nineteenth centuries.

A common thread running through the writings of major formulators of the Christian tradition including the Protestant Reformers Martin Luther, John Calvin and John Knox, is the idea that woman is inferior to man either on account of her creation from man's rib, or her role in the 'Fall' or as a 'helpmate' to man. Such patriarchal ideas extend into the twentieth century and may be seen, for instance, in the writings of the influential Protestant thinker Karl Barth. Not until the emergence of 'feminist theology' in recent times has a serious challenge been presented to negative interpretations of the Genesis texts relating to women which have dominated the Christian tradition for almost two thousand years.

The ordinary Muslim believes, as seriously as the ordinary Christian, that Adam was God's primary creation and that Eve was formed from Adam's rib, even though this myth has no basis whatever in the Qur'an, which in the context of human creation speaks always in completely egalitarian terms. In none of the thirty or so passages that describe the creation of humanity (designated by generic terms such as *'an-nas'*, *'al-insan'*, and *'bashar'*) by God in a variety of ways is there a statement that could be interpreted as asserting or suggesting that man was created prior to woman or that woman was created from man. The Qur'an notwithstanding, Muslims believe that Hawwa' (the Hebrew/Arabic counterpart of Eve) who, incidentally, is never mentioned in the Qur'an, was created from the 'crooked' rib of Adam, who is believed to be the first human being created by God. Here it needs to be mentioned that the term 'Adam' is not an Arabic term, but a Hebrew term which is a collective noun referring to the human species rather than to a male human being. In the Qur'an also, the term 'Adam' refers in twenty-one cases out of twenty-five to humanity.

If the Qur'an makes no distinction between the creation of man and woman – as it clearly does not – why do Muslims believe that Hawwa' was created from the rib of Adam? It would appear to be the case that in ways yet unresearched, the Yahwist account of woman's creation became incorporated in the Hadith literature which is the second source of the Islamic tradition (the first one being the Qur'an, which Muslims believe to be God's Word). There are six 'ahadith' (traditions attributed to the Prophet Muhammad) in the two most authoritative Hadith collections by

Imams Bukhari and Muslim, which state that woman is either created from a rib or is like a rib which is crooked and can never be straightened. Although in theory the Qur'an can never be superseded by Hadith, in the context of woman's creation this appears to have happened.

III. Was woman responsible for the 'fall' of man?

Muslims, like Christians, would generally answer this question in the affirmative, though nothing in the Qur'anic text warrants such an answer. Here it may be noted that in Genesis 3.6 the dialogue preceding the eating of the forbidden fruit is between the serpent and Eve (though Adam's presence is also indicated, as emphasized by feminist theologians), and this has been used by formulators of traditional Christianity to cast Eve into the role of tempter, deceiver and seducer of Adam. In the Qur'an, the 'Shaitan' (Satan) has no exclusive dialogue with Adam's 'zauj' (mate), nor is there any suggestion in the text that Hawwa' being tempted and deceived by the 'Shaitan', in turn tempted and deceived Adam and led to his 'Fall'.

It is difficult to overemphasize the negative impact on Christian women of the traditional interpretation of the story of the 'Fall', which has been used to perpetuate the myth of feminine evil. Through the centuries Christian women have borne the greater share of the burden of 'fallenness' which has been associated since Augustine with sexuality and the idea of original sin. In the framework of Qur'anic theology, since Adam was always meant to be God's vicegerent on earth, as stated clearly in Surah 2: *Al-Baqarah*: 30, there is no Fall from heaven to earth or any mention of original sin. Despite this, Muslims, like Christians, have often regarded women as 'the devil's gateway', finding support for their misogynistic views in 'ahadith' which though lacking in authenticity continue to be popular.

IV. Why was woman created?

The idea that woman was made not only from man but also for man has been much emphasized by traditional Christianity. The Qur'an on the other hand, emphasizes that creation as a whole is 'for just ends'. Humanity, fashioned 'in the best of moulds' comprises both women and men who are equally called upon by God to be righteous, being assured that they will be equally rewarded for their righteousness.

In spite of the Qur'anic affirmation of man-woman equality, Muslim societies, in general, have never regarded men and women as equal, particularly in the context of marriage. The alleged superiority of men to women that permeates the Islamic (as also the Christian) tradition is grounded not only in Hadith literature but also in popular interpretations of some Qur'anic passages such as Surah 4: *An-Nisa'*: 34.

Conclusion

There is hardly any doubt that women have been discriminated against by patriarchal Christianity as by patriarchal Islam. However, the re-reading and re-interpretation of significant women related Biblical and Qur'anic texts by feminist theologians has shown that it is possible to understand these texts in more than one way, and that – in fact – understanding them in egalitarian rather than in hierarchical terms is more in keeping with the belief, fundamental in both religious tradition, that God, the universal creator and sustainer, is just to all creation.

Indonesia: Living Together in a Majority Muslim Population

Judo Poerwowidagdo

I. The five principles of the Constitution

Indonesia is an archipelago, with 13,667 islands, of which more than 6,000 are inhabited. It is a country with a population of approximately 185 million. Although the majority of the people, about 85%, are Muslims, Indonesia is not an Islamic state, unlike its neighbour Malaysia, where with only about 50% of its population Muslim, Islam is declared the state religion. The Constitution of the Republic of Indonesia, known as the 1945 Constitution, guarantees freedom of religion for all citizens. However, the government through its Department of Religion recognizes only six religions, namely Islam, Protestant, Catholic, Hindhu Darma, Buddhism and Confucianism. Although the government through its Department of Religion officially recognizes only these six religions as adhered to by the Indonesian people, it also recognizes adherents of other faiths or beliefs known as 'streams of beliefs' (*aliran-aliran kepercayaan*). However, these streams of beliefs are not considered to be religions as such, but cultural manifestations. Therefore the adherents are served not by the Department of Religion but by the Directorate General of Culture, within the Department of Education and Culture.

The 1945 Constitution is based on the *Pancasila* philosophy which is written as the Preambule of the Constitution. *Pancasila* means five principles. These five principles are: 1. belief in the one supreme God; 2. just and civilized humanism; 3. unity of Indonesia; 4. the sovereignty of the people guided by inner wisdom in the unanimity arising out of deliberations among representatives; and 5. social justice for the whole people of Indonesia. Through the national consensus, decreed by the People's Consultative Assembly in 1968, *Pancasila* became the sole basis for the socio-political life of Indonesia as a nation and as a country. This implies that all social, political and even religious organizations must state in their charters or constitutions that *Pancasila* is the basis of the organization.

II. Religious life in Indonesia

Indonesian society is characterized by ethnic and cultural plurality and its ramifications. Throughout the centuries, the Indonesian archipelago has accommodated various cultural elements from India, China and Saudi Arabia as well as Western Europe. Elements of these cultural influences are still found in contemporary Indonesian society: in the language, the dress or costumes, the food, the music and dances, in the religions and the attitudes of life or the world-views of the people in general.

There are about 250 different ethnic languages. Although the Javanese (ethnic) language is spoken by a large majority of the population (more than 70 million), it was not chosen as the national language. There is only one national language, *Bahasa Indonesia* (Indonesian language), which originates from a much smaller ethnic group, but which is now spoken by all Indonesians. It has grown into a *lingua franca*, a common business language spoken during earlier centuries. The historical and cultural development of the Indonesian society cannot be separated from the influence of the religions which are currently present in Indonesia. Religious tolerance is generally practised by most Indonesians. Traditionally, Indonesian people have always been religious, in the sense that they practise one form of religion or another. Religiosity is essentially the acceptance of and adherence to a particular religious teaching or doctrine which is believed to be the only true religion which offers human salvation. Therefore the acceptance of and adherence to a particular religion implicitly implies a rejection of other religions. No other religion can be considered to be true and offer similar salvation.

This faith in a particular religion as the only true religion which promises or offers salvation invariably encourages its adherents to invite or to bring others to believe and to adhere to it. The activities of the adherents of this religion to propagate and to proclaim the religion or faith they profess are not only urged by the religious call or instruction of these 'missionary religions' such as Islam and Christianity which explicitly instructs its adherents to spread and proclaim their faith. Such activities are also motivated by an honourable wish to share the truth and the salvation offered to the 'believers'. On the basis of a similar rationale, religious adherents make efforts so that those who believe in the same religion or faith do not change or be converted to other religions. To do so would be considered an act of unpardonable sin, which according to the Islamic law is considered as '*syirk*'. Religiosity is therefore very closely related to religious propagation and religious care or nurture of the adherents of a religion. These are two things which frequently create tension among adherents of various religions in Indonesia. Legally however, conversion from one religion to another is possible since the religious freedom guaranteed by the 1945 Constitution, gives room not only for the practice of religions but also for religious conversion. Although religious plurality bears the potential for conflicts, in Indonesian contemporary history there has never been any war between religions or religious adherents. Religion as a source of social conflicts in Indonesia has been reduced or contained because of the policy of 'religious tolerance' which is promoted and tightly held by the Government.

III. Inter-religious dialogues

From 1972 to 1977 the Department of Religion conducted a programme of inter-religious dialogues twenty-three times in twenty-one cities throughout the country. From 1976 to 1978, eight case studies seminar/workshops were held in seven regions, involving the co-operation and working together of various religious scholars and experts, and since 1977 several programmes of co-operation in study camps, social activities and dialogues have been held involving the students of theology of the Protestant Theological Seminary, the Institute of Philosophy and Theology (Seminary) of the Roman Catholic Church and the state Islamic Institute. These programmes of inter-religious dialogues are held both at the national level and at the regional/provincial level. The topics discussed in such inter-religious dialogues include issues of inter-relations or religious adherents and common important issues, such as national development, etc.

One of the concrete results of these inter-religious dialogues was the establishment of the National Inter-Religious Council (*Wadah Musyawarah Antar Umat Beragama Nasional*) in 1979. This council is a forum for the discussion of religious policies which will have some bearing on inter-religious relations, and can act to defuse any potential or actual inter-religious conflicts. In the development of religious life in Indonesia, each of the six recognized religions has its top or national organizational structure. For the Muslims it is the Council of Ulamas in Indonesia (*Majelis Ulama Indonesia*), for the Protestants the Communion of Churches in Indonesia (*Persekutuan Gereja-Gereja di Indonesia*), for the Roman Catholics the Indonesian Bishops Conference (*Konperensi Wali*

Agung Gereja Indonesia), for the Hindus the Hindu Dharma Council (*Parisada Hindu Dharma*), for the Buddhists the Great Council of Buddhist Religion in Indonesia (*Majelis Agung Agama Budha Indonesia*), and for the Confucianists the High Council of Confucian Religion in Indonesia (*Majelis Tinggi Agama Kong Hu Cu di Indonesia*). The Inter-Religious Council consists of the representatives of these top, national religious organizations while the Government is represented through the Minister of Religion or his representative.

Through these various fora of inter-religious dialogues the Government has promoted the principle of 'peaceful and harmonious relationship' known as *Tiga Kerukunan*, which means three peaceful and harmonious relationships: 1. peaceful and harmonious relationship inter (among) religions; 2. peaceful and harmonious relationship intra religion; and 3. peaceful and harmonious relationship between religions and the government. With this principle of peaceful and harmonious relationship, it is expected that there will be no serious conflicts on religious matters among the parties concerned. It is of course recognized that differences do exist. However, should tension arise because of these differences it should not result in open conflicts but must be resolved peacefully.

IV. Inter-religious life in the community

Inter-religious dialogue is more common at the family or neighbourhood (grass root) level in the form of living peacefully and harmoniously together. It is not rare to find a family or household where the members belong to different religions. It could be the husband or the wife, the children or other members of the household who belong to a different religion from the rest of the family. Many households consist of the parents and children plus any number of the extended family: grandparents, cousins or nephews/nieces, aunts or uncles and even household helpers, who are outsiders, etc. Inter-religious marriages are not uncommon. In many parts of Indonesia, where the clan or *marga* system of family relationship exists, none of the clan or *marga* can or would claim that all the members belong to the same religion.

In many regions, where members of the community belong to more than one religion, one can witness a life full of tolerance, manifested not only in an attitude of mutual respect and consideration, but also in readiness to help each other in the various activities which relate to religion, such as building a mosque or a church, celebrating Christmas or the festival of Qur'an recital (*Musabaqoh Tilawatil Qur'an*). One may expect even more co-operation in other spheres of community social life. It is very common for neighbours who belong to different religions to visit each other during religious celebrations or holidays, such as Idulfitr or Christmas.

The daily environment of religious plurality in the community helps the children to grow up with religious tolerance. In schools children sit in the same class with others having different religious affiliation. For most people, adherence to a particular religious life in general is the product of social environment, and not the result of a free choice. Children who are born into a Muslim family, raised in an Islamic community, will generally become Muslims. Similarly, children who are born of Christian parents, raised in a Christian family environment will become Christians. This does not mean, however, that there is no possibility of being converted to another faith or religion. Those who change their religious adherence may do so because of an unsatisfactory religious life in their own religion, but others may be motivated by a variety of other reasons. The population of Indonesia is concentrated in the Island of Java, where approximately 100 million people live. The Muslim population of Java have been described by some scholars variantly as '*santri*' and '*abangan*'. The '*santri*' are those Muslims who fervently practice the Islamic teaching and observe faithfully the Islamic laws, while the '*abangan*', the large majority, are those who have limited knowledge and practice of Islam, many of whom are just nominally Muslims and are known as 'statistical Muslims'.

V. Development in self-perception

Muslims in Indonesia, especially in Java, have experienced a development in self-perception which is caused by the struggle with concrete social and political issues and their moral implications. Therefore Islam in Java is different from Islam in the Middle East. The '*santri*' culture cannot be compared with Islam culture in the Middle East. Some Arabs may consider that the Islam of the Javanese is not in accordance with the Qur'an and the Hadith. On the other hand, the Javanese may consider that the Islam of the Arabs is not in line with the *sunnah* of the Prophet. Christians in Indonesia in general are experiencing a similar change in self-perception, as they confront the social and political realities in Indonesian society. The historical and cultural contexts as well as the socio-political matrix of the Christian churches have caused the churches to develop a theology of 'double wrestle'. Christians are citizens of the kingdom of God, and yet they are called to be citizens of this world (Indonesia) and must live together in harmony with other citizens. Islam and Christianity, like Hinduism and Buddhism which preceded them, can survive in Indonesian society by adopting a process of continuous 'dialogue' with their contexts.

VI. The importance of peace among the religions

As a new nation (which proclaimed its independence at the end of the Second World War) and like many other developing nations, Indonesian society faces three intertwined issues, namely: 1. the problem of nation building (national integration); 2. the problem of political stability; and 3. the problem of economic development. Nation-building requires political stability and economic development. Political stability can be achieved if the threat of national disintegration is eliminated and at the same time economic development enjoys a relatively steady progress. Economic development cannot be achieved without political stability and national unity. History has taught us that the cost of open religious conflict is high and the ultimate consequences are grave indeed. Therefore, peace and harmony among people of different religious adherence is of paramount importance and should be continually nurtured and developed.

The Indonesian situation is an example *par excellence* of living together by peoples of different faiths. First, there is the constitutional guarantee of religious freedom, which allows conversion from one religion to another. Secondly, religious tolerance is promoted and tightly held by the government, supported by programmes of inter-religious dialogues involving all adherents of the various religions. Thirdly, the principle of active peaceful and harmonious relationship, nor merely passive peaceful co-existence, is widely practised and promoted. Fourthly, a national forum for the discussion of religious policies which affect inter-religious relations, and which can act to diffuse any potential or actual inter-religious conflict, is established.

In all religions, to love other human beings is an important element in understanding the various social activities which strengthen peaceful and harmonious relationships and reinforce social solidarity. The cohesion of a society is very much dependent on this ability to understand and to internalize, to love other human beings, which is rooted in religion.

II · Threats

Islam, the One and the Many: Unity and Diversity in a Global Tradition

John Renard

In their views of Islam, both Muslims and non-Muslims seem on the whole to gravitate toward the notion that all Muslims are really the same, but they do so for very different reasons. Non-Muslim (especially European and American) images of a monolithic Islam often arise out of a fear of the unknown that encourages oversimplification in dealing with 'the other'. That fear is in turn exacerbated by long-standing stereotypes of Muslims as bellicose and generally given to religiously motivated and sanctioned violence.

For their part, Muslims tend for several reasons to dismiss the notion that there are varieties of Islam. One is that their tradition's characterizations of Christian disunity poses an unacceptable image of a religious community; another is that their own understanding of, and wish for, a truly global community of Muslims leaves no room whatsoever for any significant diversity within it.

If non-Muslims' consistent attribution of a seamless unity to Islam rests on an unjustifiably negative reading of Muslims as humanly homogeneous, that of Muslims is built on an equally uncritical idealization of Islam as religiously uniform. The first characterization is unfair, the second unrealistic. One needs a way to understand both the religious unity and the human and cultural diversity of the world's nearly one billion Muslims.

I. The notion of *umma* as global community

To begin, let us look briefly at the Islamic tradition's deep-seated sense of, and desire for, global all-inclusive unity. Since the very earliest days, Islamic sources have emphasized a strong sense of the universal purpose and destiny of the faith proclaimed by Muhammad. That tradition and its adherents have maintained a common belief in the transcendent unity of God and in the prophetic office and function of the final and definitive Messenger of God.

With respect to its range of religious practice, Islam is often characterized as standing upon the five firm pillars of orthopraxy, namely: ritual prayer five times a day facing Mecca; pilgrimage once in a lifetime, given sufficient health and means; fasting from sunrise to sunset during Ramadan, the ninth lunar month; almsgiving as a way of sharing one's blessings and acknowledging God as the Giver of all things; and living out the basic profession of faith: there is no deity but God, and Muhammad is the Messenger of God. One often hears Muslims assert that given these basic symbols of unity, any and all appearances of diversity and disunity are merely that – appearances, and not worth discussing further. Perhaps so, from a very minimalistic perspective. But when one sets out to understand Islam and all its manifestations in greater detail, one quickly discovers that there are indeed significant variations.

II. Unity within diversity

We shall examine that unity within diversity from several points of view. First, two fundamentally divergent interpretations of Islam's sacred history have given rise to the now classic distinction between *Sunni* and *Shi'i* Muslims. Second, variations in regional interpretations and, hence, in the implementation of Islamic revealed law have built a legacy of various 'schools' of, or methodological approaches to, religious law. Third, Islam's interactions with the multiple cultural matrices in which it has taken root across the globe have likewise made it useful and even necessary to discern within given cultural contexts how Muslims manifest their beliefs in a variety of ways. Fourth, returning to the broader scope of Islam as a global phenomenon, one can describe a variety of styles of professing, living and interpreting Islam that seem to cut across cultural boundaries. And finally, we look very briefly at several sectarian developments of ostensibly Islamic origin, but of questionable authenticity.

1. Diversity and the interpretation of history

Perhaps the most widely known manifestation of diversity within the global community of Muslims has taken the form of the division between *Sunni* and *Shi'i* Muslims. One can cite numerous instances, say within the United States, of *Sunni* and *Shi'i* Muslims sharing the same place of prayer and engaging in religious discussion together. Some will conclude that any perceived differences between members of the two groups are purely incidental. Some may observe further that one will scarcely see members of different Christian denominations worshipping together, finding here proof that Christians are genuinely divided while Muslims are divided only nominally. But we must acknowledge two large realities here. First, just as all Christians share a core of basic beliefs, so do all Muslims. And second, just as there are *de facto*, observable secondary differences in Christian expression of faith and practice, so also does the world community of Muslims exhibit undeniable variations within itself.

Diversity in this instance arises in large measure from two significantly different interpretations of crucial events in Islam's early history – different theologies of history, one might say. Upon Muhammad's death, in 632, the Muslim community faced its greatest crisis to date: how to ensure the legitimate succession to the Prophet. Two schools of thought began to emerge. The majority held that Muhammad had not explicitly appointed a successor before he died, and that it fell to the elders among Muhammad's companions to choose one from among themselves to serve as the first Caliph (viceroy, successor). They chose the venerable Abu Bakr, one of Muhammad's fathers-in-law. Abu Bakr served for two years; when he died, Umar was chosen, and he in turn was followed by Uthman. The majority came to be known as the 'people of the *sunna* (example of the Prophet) and the assembly', *Sunni* for short. An example of the authority to which *Sunni* Muslims have turned as evidence of the correctness of their stand is a *hadith* (saying) of Muhammad in which he observed that his community would be divided into seventy-three sects, only one of which would be saved. Asked which would see salvation, Muhammad referred to the followers of the '*sunna* and the Assembly', which he then defined further as that which he and his companions practised.

A minority position held that Muhammad had indeed designated his cousin and son-in-law Ali as his Caliph. The first three successors backed by the majority were, they insisted, usurpers. The supporters or partisans (*shi'a*) of Ali pressed their case, and after the murder of Uthman, Ali became Caliph – the fourth according to majority reckoning, the first legitimate one from the *Shi'i* perspective. According to the *Shi'i* interpretation, the lawful successor to the Prophet must be designated by his living predecessor and be of the family of Muhammad. Classical *Shi'i* theology came to recognize a line of spiritual and biological descendants of the Prophet, numbering variously five or seven or twelve depending on the particular *Shi'i* branch in question. One could describe the *Shi'i* interpretation of history in general as millenialist, with its expectation of the return or renewed manifestation of a long-concealed spiritual leader who will usher in an age of perfect justice for all.

Today approximately eighty to ninety per cent of Muslims are *Sunni*, and the remainder *Shi'i*, these mostly of the branch known as Twelvers. The latter comprise the vast majority of Iranians and a slight majority of Iraqis. Some of the most significant differences between *Sunni* and *Shi'i* approaches to religious matters have to do with structures of authority and with certain devotional practices. With regard to the former, *Shi'ism* has developed a more hierarchical approach to religious authority; as for the latter, an example of a distinctively *Shi'i* practice is the observance of pious visitation of the tombs of the holy ones, the Imams, and commemoration of the redemptive suffering of the Family of Muhammad.

2. *Diversity in the implementation of revealed law*

As the Muslim community spread into new territories beyond Arabia, it came into contact with a wide range of cultures and already ancient legal systems, both religious and secular. During Muhammad's lifetime the administration of the revealed law (*shari'a*) as embodied progressively in the Qur'an and the Prophet's *ad hoc* pronouncements (*hadiths*) remained relatively uncomplicated. But in ever new cultural, ethnic and social settings, implementation of that law posed a number of challenges. Beginning in the early eighth century, there developed a range of legal methodologies. All Muslims agreed substantially that Qur'an and *hadith* constituted the bedrock of religious law. But what was one to do if a question not addressed in either of those sources arose? First resort was to be sought in the actual practice (*sunna*) of the local community – a consensus (*ijma'*) that amounts to a sort of *sensus fidelium*. But if actual practice offered no basis for ruling, one might as a final resort appeal to the informed analogical reasoning (*qiyas*) of legal scholars.

Among *Sunni* Muslims four of the ancient legal schools have survived into modern times, varying especially with respect to the acceptability of having recourse to legal reasoning. At one end of the spectrum stands the Hanbali school (or *madhhab*), the most cautious, methodologically speaking; its sphere of influence is limited largely to Saudi Arabia. At the opposite end is the Hanafi school, dominant, for example, in Turkey, India and Pakistan. In between are the Maliki school, of greatest importance in North Africa, and the Shafi'i school, now important in South East Asia and parts of Egypt.

Shi'i law has also seen the development of schools, the most important of which differ as to whether a Muslim may interpret the sources directly or must seek the ruling of a living legal scholar. The currently dominant Mujtahidi (or Usuli) school, with its emphasis on the authoritative ruling of the *mujtahid* (one who exercises independent investigation), has at least temporarily superseded the Akhbaris. Integral to the initial structure of the Islamic Republic of Iran, and related in part to the success of the revolution that overthrew the Shah in 1979, was the overriding authority of Imam Khumayni as the supreme lawgiver.

3. Diversity and cultural matrices

A third measure of variety has to do with the range of ways Islam has interacted with cultures. One may profitably speak here of the dual phenomena of Islamization and indigenization. Islamization is the process by which the religious tradition of Islam becomes a crucial influence on a culture or ethnic group or region. Indigenization is the process by which a culture, ethnic group, or region puts its own stamp on Islam. Taken together, these two processes can help one understand how and to what extent Moroccan Islam is both similar to and different from Indonesian Islam.

Here again one finds that many Muslims prefer to dismiss such differences as meaningless; Muslims are Muslims and it does not matter where they live. In fact it matters a great deal, not so much in the content of their basic beliefs or in the practice of the essential duties, as in the ways Islam figures in people's sense of identity. In Indonesia, for example, the character of Islam has much to do with the nation's long history of religious diversity as well as with its decision, upon gaining independence, not to declare Islamic *shari'a* the state legal system.

Within a particular culture, too, one can discern important differences in the ways Muslims see themselves and one another. In Indonesia (on the island of Java in particular), for example, Muslims have traditionally fallen into three quite distinct and widely recognized groupings. Priyayi Muslims retain the most pronounced ties to their aristocratic backgrounds complete with heavy Indian courtly and religious influences. At the other end of the spectrum are the Santris, the most self-consciously Islamic segment of the population, who cultivate a sense of belonging to a wider community of Muslims. As a symbol of solidarity with the Islamic Middle Eastern lands of origin, the use of Arabic for religious purposes is particularly important to the Santris. In between are the majority Abangan, whose Islam remains heavily tinged with local traditions. One could cite analogous intra-cultural diversity in a number of other important Islamized areas as well.

4. Attitudinal diversity across cultural boundaries

Returning to the notion of Islam as a global phenomenon, we come finally to several indicators of cross-cultural diversity as well. Here we are dealing rather broadly with a range of attitudes and intellectual postures rather than with specific devotional or practical variants. Sometimes referred to by such labels as religio-cultural styles, for example, these variations are rather elusive and conjectural, for they do not simply wrap around neatly circumscribed populations of Muslims. One must take these characterizations as such with a grain of salt. Here I propose four varieties of religious attitude: the traditionalist or conservative; the revivalist; the adaptationist; and the personalist.

Probably the vast majority of the world's Muslims are traditionalist or religiously conservative. Islam and its historic institutions are for them a firm anchor in a sea of change and turmoil. In general, traditionalists have no burning desire to stir the political pot or to foment revolutions. Like most members of most religious traditions, perhaps, they look to their faith community to provide a sense of stability and order, preferring even religiously reprehensible governance to the possibility of anarchy.

An increasingly vocal segment of many Islamic populations in several parts of the world are those religious activists I shall call revivalists. These are Muslims who want to see firmly religious values returned to what they regard as the pride of place they once enjoyed in Islam. Their goal is in some ways highly idealistic, but many are motivated by genuine religious zeal. One must take care to distinguish between such idealistic activists and those violence-prone individuals and groups so frequently referred to as fundamentalists.

One often hears the term 'fundamentalists' used, misleadingly, to describe Muslims who willingly engage in terrorist acts, such as hostage takings, assassinations, suicide bombings and the like. Print and electronic media regularly characterize suspects in such incidents as fanatical or extremist fundamentalist Muslims, largely because they are often heard shouting 'God is Supreme', calling for a *jihad* (unfortunately often translated as 'holy war') against the enemies of Islam, and generally employing ostensibly religious rhetoric.

I use the term revivalist here in preference to fundamentalist, and refer to them as Muslims because their basic beliefs and practices place them squarely within the Islamic tradition. Needless to say, especially in countries in which the average criminal suspect would rarely if ever be singled out as Jewish or Christian, much current media practice causes untold grief to the vast majority of peaceable Muslims who are horrified by the parading of mindless violence under the banner of Islam.

By no means all religiously activist Muslims would counsel the use of violent means in any case. There are many disaffected, mostly younger, Muslims who desperately want change and would like to see Islamic values given a chance at the level of government, but who are dedicated to bringing about such changes by political means. In addition, it is important to note that much of what is labelled fundamentalist Islam has little or nothing to do with Islamic values as such, and is the product of a revolutionary, rather than a truly religious, fervour. It remains true, nevertheless, that Islam does indeed provide sanction for struggle (*jihad*) against any widely recognized injustice. Islam is not alone in that regard, but one has to corrupt its sources to find in them any hint of approval of terrorism.

A third attitude is the adaptationist, though some might prefer the terms modernist or reformist, while many more conservative Muslims would label it Westernism or a sell-out to colonialist values. Adaptationists are those who seek to promote understanding of Islam as wholly compatible with, perhaps even ultimately responsible for, the best in the advancement of every sphere of human knowledge and inventiveness. Muslim majorities have often criticized the attitude either for excessive reliance on the use of reason (as in the case of the classical thought of the Mu'tazilites), or for seeming to pander to non-Islamic interests (such as many have identified as modern 'Western' imperialism and colonialism).

In the personalist attitude one finds a thread that has run through a variety of developments within Islam over the centuries. One sees the attitude in the unquestioning allegiance of a religious seeker to a spiritual guide in one of Islam's religious confraternities, as well as in the absolute devotion of many revolutionary Iranians to Imam Khumayni. Where traditionalists seek stable uniformity in community, revivalists hope for a renewed centrality of Islamic religious rule and moral values, and adaptationists strive to demonstrate rationally Islam's compatibility with the larger picture of human progress, personalists elevate the authority of a charismatic leader to the highest level.

III. Sectarian developments of Islamic origin

Finally, what of those groups of people who identify themselves as Muslims, but whose Muslim identity the vast majority of Muslims appears to question or even to deny outright? A number of such developments have occurred especially since the nineteenth century in various parts of the world. Of mediaeval origin are the Druze, originally an offshoot of a Sevener or Isma'ili *Shi'i* dynasty called the Fatimids of Egypt. Modern times have witnessed the beginnings of the Baha'i and Ahmadiyya movements. And in the twentieth century, both the Nation of Islam and the Moorish Science Temple have arisen in the United States of America. Of these movements, all but the Druze and Baha'i insist strongly that they are truly Muslims. Just a quick glance at some of the key doctrinal tenets of these groups, however, leaves little doubt as to why mainstream Muslims consider them outside the authentic Islamic fold. One finds, for example, denial of the resurrection, belief in a prophetic mission after Muhammad, little or no emphasis on daily ritual prayer or other essential practices, and so forth.

In the final analysis, one can discern in that massive worldwide phenomenon known as Islam both unity and diversity. On the one hand Islam as a religious tradition offers its adherents a high degree of cohesiveness and identity as members of a global community of faith. On the other, Islam continues to reflect the striking cultural, ethnic and attitudinal diversity of the people who call themselves Muslims.

The Threat of Islam: Myth or Reality?

John L. Esposito

If the 1980s were dominated by a fear of Iran's export of its revolution, the 1990s have enhanced the spectre of a global Islamic threat.[1] The many faces of contemporary Islam have tended to be subsumed under the monolith of 'Islamic fundamentalism', which has become equated with violence and terrorism. Memories of the Ayatollah Khomeini's denunciation of America as the 'Great Satan', the condemnation of Salman Rushdie, author of *The Satanic Verses*, hostage taking in Lebanon, Saddam Hussein's call for a *jihad* in the Persian Gulf War of 1991, bombings in New York (World Trade Center), Cairo and southern Lebanon, fears of an organized, co-ordinated effort by Iran and Sudan to foster and spread Islamic radicalism – all have reinforced images of Islam as a militant, expansionist religion, rabidly anti-American and intent upon war with the West. At the same time, attacks by Egyptian extremists upon Coptic Christians in Egypt, the impact of Islamic governments in the Sudan and Pakistan, and Muslim-Christian communal warfare in Lebanon have been sources of grave concern to Christian communities.

I. Roots of concern and misunderstanding

Ancient rivalries as well as modern-day conflicts have so accentuated differences as completely to obscure the shared monotheistic roots and vision of the Judaeo-Christian-Islamic tradition. Despite many common beliefs and values, throughout history, Muslim-Christian relations have often been overshadowed by conflict as the armies and missionaries of Islam and Christendom have been locked in a struggle for power and for souls. This confrontation has ranged from the fall of the early Byzantine (eastern Roman) empire before the armies of Islam in the seventh century to the fierce battles and polemics of the Crusades, the expulsion of the 'Moors' from Spain and the Inquisition, the Ottoman threat to overrun

Europe, European (Christian) colonial expansion and domination in the eighteenth and nineteenth centuries, the political and cultural challenge of the super-powers (America and the Soviet Union) in the latter half of the twentieth century, the creation of the state of Israel, the competition of Christian and Muslim missionaries for converts in Africa today and the challenge of the contemporary reassertion of Islam or 'Islamic fundamentalism'. As a result, Islam's relationship with the West has often been marked less by understanding than by mutual ignorance and stereotyping, confrontation and conflict.

1. The challenge of the contemporary Islamic resurgence

Islam re-emerged as a potent global force during the 1970s and 1980s.[2] The power and vitality of contemporary Islamic revivalism is rooted in a broad-based phenomenon, the reassertion of Islam in Muslim personal and political life.[3] While Islam remained a widespread presence in Muslim societies, in recent years it has proven to be a dynamic and vital socio-political force in Muslim societies. Many Muslims became more personally religiously observant regarding prayer, fasting, dress and behaviour. Islam also emerged as a major ideological force and alternative in political and social life. Muslim governments and opposition movements turned to or had to contend with the greater role of religion in public life. Islamic symbolism and discourse became a primary source of legitimacy and popular mobilization. Islamic organizations proliferated and developed as significant political and social actors.

A review of contemporary Islamic politics challenges perceptions of a monolithic 'Islamic fundamentalism' or pan-Islamic threat. State implementation of Islam has varied markedly in terms of its forms of government, domestic programmes and foreign policies. Monarchs, military rulers, presidents and clergy have ruled governments as diverse as Saudi Arabia's conservative monarchy, Libya's populist socialist state, Iran's clerical republic and Sudan and Pakistan's military regimes. Similarly, while some have enjoyed close ties with the West, others have been regarded as a threat to Western interests. Within specific countries, contending voices and groups have vied for power in the name of Islam.

Modern Islamic organizations and movements have been the driving force behind the dynamic spread of the Islamic resurgence. They have also been the focal point or embodiment of the Islamic threat in the eyes of Western governments. For some, Islamic movements represent an authentic alternative to corrupt exhausted and ineffectual regimes. For many others, they are a destabilizing force – demagogues who will employ any tactic to gain power. The violence and terrorism perpetrated by groups in Lebanon and Egypt with names like the Party of God, Holy War, Army of God, Salvation from Hell, and the Gamaa Islamiyya (Islamic Group) embody a 'Sacred Rage' that have become all too familiar.[4] Yet, the reality is far more complex and diverse than its popular image. While a minority are vocal violent revolutionaries, the majority (the Muslim Brotherhoods of Egypt and Jordan, the Islamic Salvation Front in Algeria, the Renaissance Party in Tunisia, the Jamaat-i-Islami in Pakistan, the Nahdatul Ulama and Muhamadiyya in Indonesia, and ABIM and PAS in Malaysia) work within the political system and seek change from below through a gradual process of reform. Many have espoused political liberalization and democratization.

2. *From the periphery to the centre: mainstream revivalism*

If throughout much of the 1970s and 80s Islamic revivalism or fundamentalism was equated with radical extremist groups on the fringes of society, in the 1990s it is clear that the resurgence of Islam is far more complex. Islamic revivalism is a broad-based religio-social movement, part of mainstream Muslim society. The presence and appeal of a more pronounced Islamic orientation is to be found among the middle and lower classes, men and women, educated and uneducated, professionals and workers. While small radical groups continue to exist and engage in acts of violence and terrorism, in many Muslim countries Islamic activism has become institutionalized, working and prospering within the system. A new class of modern educated but Islamically oriented elites has emerged working alongside, and at times in opposition to, their secular counterparts. Their goal is the transformation of society through the Islamic formation of individuals and through social and political action. Dawah (Call) societies work in social services (hospitals, clinics, legal aid societies), in economic projects (Islamic banks, investment houses, insurance companies), in education (schools, child care centres, youth camps), and in religious publishing and broadcasting. Islamic activists have become part and parcel of the political process. They have participated in national and local elections, scoring an impressive victory in Algeria's municipal and parliamentary elections and emerging as the chief opposition in Egypt, Tunisia and Jordan. Activists serve in cabinet level positions in Sudan, Jordan, Pakistan, Iran and Malaysia.

Ironically, the extent to which the resurgence of Islam has become part of mainstream Muslim life and society has led many to see it as an even greater threat. In many Muslim countries, state institutions are now complemented or challenged by Islamically orientated schools, clinics, hospitals, banks and social services. Their success in providing much-needed services is often taken by regimes as an implicit, if not explicit, critique or threat, underscoring their limitations and failures. Similarly, the emergence of an alternative elite, with a modern education but more Islamically orientated, offers an alternative view of politics and society that challenges the Western, secular presuppositions, life-styles, power and privileges of entrenched elites.

II. Islam and the West: challenge or threat?

Much as Western observers in the past retreated to polemics and stereotypes of Arabs, Turks or Muslims in proclaiming pan-Arab and pan-Islamic threats, today we are witnessing the perpetuation or creation of a new myth. Islam has come to be viewed as a triple threat: political, demographic and religio-social. The impending confrontation between Islam and the West is presented as part of an historical pattern of Muslim belligerency and aggression. Past images of a Christian West turning back the threat of Muslim armies to overrun the West are conjured up and linked to current realities, warning of 'religious Stalinists' bent on an Islamic 'crusade' against the West, inspired and supported by Iran, 'the new comintern'.[5] Some speak of a global Islamic uprising, of Muslims in the heartland and in the periphery of the Muslim world rising up in revolt: a 'new "arc of crisis" . . . another great movement is going on as well, unnoticed but just as portentous: a global intifada'.[6]

1. A demographic threat?

The nature of the Islamic threat is intensified by the linkage of the political and the demographic. Thus, Patrick Buchanan could write in 'Rising Islam May Overwhelm the West' that while the West finds itself 'negotiating for hostages with Shiite radicals who hate and detest us', their Muslim 'co-religionists are filling up the countries of the West'. The Muslim threat becomes global in nature, says Buchanan, as Muslims in Europe, the former Soviet Union and America 'proliferate and prosper'.

Events in the West continue to reinforce the perspective of an impending *demographic threat*. The presence of significant Muslim minority populations, from the Middle East, Asia and Africa, puts strains on the social fabric of European societies in Great Britain, Germany and France among others. Anti-Arab/Muslim sentiment in Western Europe is part of a growing xenophobia. Similarly, the bombing of the World Trade Center and subsequent indictments of Shaykh Omar Abdur Rahman and others for conspiracy to engage in urban terrorism has focussed attention on America's sizeable Muslim population and raised immigration issues.

2. Islam and democracy compatible?

The participation of Islamic organizations in electoral politics, using ballots not bullets, has ironically made them an even more formidable threat to regimes in the Muslim world and some in the West. The justification for the condemnation and suppression of Islamic movements was that they were violent extremists, small non-representative groups on the margins of society, who refused to work within the system and as such were a threat to society and regional stability. Those who once dismissed their claims as unrepresentative and who denounced their radicalism as a threat to the system now accuse them of an attempt to 'hi-jack democracy'. These fears have been expressed by Western political commentators and policy-makers and exploited by authoritarian rulers in Tunisia and Algeria. This mentality caused many in the West to be silent when the Algerian military intervened, nullified legitimately held elections, and imprisoned and repressed the Islamic Salvation Front.

Incipient democratization movements in the Middle East and the broader Muslim world and the participation of Islamic movements in the electoral process raise the question: are Islam and democracy compatible?[7] Like Judaism and Christianity, Islam is capable of multiple interpretations; it has been used to support democracy and dictatorship. The twentieth century has witnessed both tendencies. While some leaders of Islamic movements have spoken out against democracy and a parliamentary system of government, their negative reaction has often been part of the general rejection of European colonial influence and a defence of Islam against further penetration of and dependence on the West rather than a wholesale rejection of democracy.

3. Differing Muslim viewpoints

There are differing Muslim viewpoints regarding the meaning of democracy, but historically there have in fact been different interpretations or models of democracy. However, an Islamic rationale or basis for the acceptance of democratic institutions and values, the Islamization of democracy, has been based upon a modern process of reinterpretation (*ijtihad*) of traditional Islamic concepts of political deliberation or consultation (*shura*), community consensus (*ijma*), and personal interpretation (*ijtihad*) or reinterpretation to support notions of parliamentary democracy, representative elections and religious reform. Islamic movements have used democracy and human rights to critique autocratic rulers as 'un-Islamic', to call for democratic elections and greater political participation in Tunisia, Algeria, Egypt, Kuwait, Morocco, Pakistan, Kashmir, Indonesia and Bangladesh.

III. Tensions between a Western and an Islamic view

However, differences between Western notions of democracy and the Islamic tradition exist. In Islamized forms of democracy, popular sovereignty is in theory to be subordinated to divine sovereignty; God's immutable law cannot be altered by human desire or whim. What this would mean in practice has varied widely from those who demand the direct implementation of classical Islamic law, others who call for the reformulation of Islamic law, and still others who believe it is sufficient that no law be contrary to the Qur'an.

1. The problem of tolerance

The record of Islamic experiments in Pakistan, Iran and the Sudan raises serious questions about the willingness of Islamically orientated governments to tolerate dissent and respect the status and rights of women and non-Muslim minorities, the nature of citizenship and the extent of their participation in the government and society.[8] Similar issues faced Christianity in the past. Indeed, until Vatican II some experts on political development believed that democracy/modern pluralism and Roman Catholicism were incompatible.

Tensions and clashes between Muslims and non-Muslim communities have increased in recent years: the Copts in Egypt, Baha'i in Iran, Chinese in Malaysia, Christians in the Sudan and Pakistan. Often non-Muslim minorities such as Christians in Egypt, the Sudan and Pakistan or the Ahmadiyya of Pakistan are regarded as having co-operated in the past and benefitted from European colonial rule. Similarly, Copts in Egypt, Chinese in Malaysia, Baha'i in Iran and Ahmadiyya in Pakistan, who tend to be perceived as more advanced educationally and economically, have encountered resentment and discrimination. Reactionary religious leaders have found it easy to mobilize or incite their followers against minorities, viewed as disproportionately successful, who have become the targets for pent up socioeconomic frustrations.

2. The status of 'non-believers'

According to Islamic law, non-Muslims belong to a class of citizens, the *dhimmi* ('protected'), who constitute their own community. In exchange for their allegiance to the state and payment of a poll tax, they are free to practise their faith and are governed by their religious leaders and laws in matters of worship, private life, education and family laws. However enlightened this position was in the past as compared to Christianity's view and treatment of 'non-believers', by modern standards it would constitute a second-class citizenship. Most modern Muslim states have granted equality of citizenship to all regardless of religious faith. However, the contemporary resurgence has resurrected pressures to reassert legally the often widespread traditional attitude towards non-Muslims which, though changed by modern legislation, has remained operative in the minds and outlooks of many Muslims.

A modern, liberal, secular pluralistic approach is contested in many quarters today by those who argue that the state's Islamic ideology requires a commitment to Islam. This would preclude non-Muslims from holding key posts in government, the legislature, judiciary and military which formulate and implement the ideology of the state. Despite modern constitutional reforms, Islamic organizations like the Muslim Brotherhood and the Jamaat-i-Islami and many religious leaders have continued to teach and preach a restricted role for non-Muslims.

Without a reinterpretation of classical Islamic legal doctrines regarding non-Muslim citizens as 'protected people' (*dhimmi*), an Islamic ideologically-orientated state would at best be a limited democratic state with a weak pluralistic profile. Its ideological orientation could restrict the participation of non-Muslims in key government positions as well as the existence of political parties that represent competing ideologies or orientations: secular or religious.

Only time will tell whether the espousal of democracy by many contemporary Islamic movements and their participation in the electoral process are simply a means to power or a truly embraced end/goal. Based on the record thus far, one can expect that where Islamic movements come into power, like many governments in the Middle East, secular as well as 'Islamic', issues of political pluralism and human rights will remain a source of considerable tension and conflict until time and experience have enabled the development of new political traditions and institutions.

3. More a challenge than a threat

Contemporary Islam is more a challenge than a threat. It challenges the West to avoid reducing the richness and diversity of Islam and the Muslim experience to a monolithic threat. Followers of Judaism and Christianity are challenged to become aware of the faith of Islam, to acknowledge their Muslim brothers and sisters as children of Abraham, and to distinguish between Islam and its exploitation by extremists much as it demands that others do so when confronted by the violence and fanaticism of Christian and Jewish extremist groups. Political Islam challenges the conventional Western secular world-view. Because Islamic activists reject the established political and intellectual order, the unquestioned acceptance of whose norms as self-evident truths often borders on a 'secular fundamentalism', Islamic activists are often *a priori* dismissed as 'abnormal', deviant, irrational, extremist. The challenge of contemporary Islamic revivalism to the political and intellectual establishment is easily transformed into a threat.

Muslim governments are challenged to be more responsive to popular demands for political liberalization and greater popular participation, to tolerate rather than repress opposition movements (including Islamic organizations and parties) and build viable democratic institutions. Political Islam is itself challenged, challenged by its own rhetoric and message to be self-critical: to live up to the standards and principles it espouses and demands of others; to avoid and denounce the excesses that are committed by governments or movements that identify themselves as Islamic; and finally, to take or share responsibility, as well as blame the West, for the failures of Muslim societies. At the same time, Western powers are challenged to stand by the democratic values they embody and to recognize authentic populist movements and the right of the people to determine the nature of their governments and leadership whether they choose a secular or a more Islamically orientated path. The twenty-first century will test our ability to distinguish between Islamic movements that are a threat and those that represent legitimate indigenous attempts to reform and redirect their societies.[9]

Notes

1. This article draws on more previous writing, in particular my *The Islamic Threat: Myth or Reality?*, New York 1993.

2. For studies of the Islamic resurgence, see Yvonne Y. Haddad, John O. Voll and John L. Esposito, *The Contemporary Islamic Revival: A Critical Survey and Bibliography* New York 1991; John L. Esposito, *Islam and Politics*, Syracuse, NY 1991; John L. Esposito (ed.), *Islam in Asia: Religion, Politics & Society*, New York 1987; James P. Piscatori (ed.), *Islam in the Political Process*, Cambridge 1983; and Nazih Ayubi, *Political Islam: Religion and Politics in the Arab World*, London 1991.

3. See John L. Esposito, *Islam and Politics*, Syracuse, NY [3]1991; Shireen Hunter (ed.), *The Politics of Islamic Revivalism*, Bloomington, Indiana 1988, and James P. Piscatori (ed.), *Islam in the Political Process*, Cambridge 1983.

4. Robin Wright, *Sacred Rage: The Wrath of Militant Islam*, New York 1985.

5. Charles Krauthammer, 'Iran: Orchestrator of Disaster', *Washington Post*, 1 January 1993; Morton Zuckerman, 'Beware of Religious Stalinists', *US News and World Report*, 22 March 1993, 80; Bernard Lewis, 'Roots of Muslim Rage', *Atlantic Monthly* 226:3 (September 1990).

6. Charles Krauthammer, 'The New Crescent of Crisis: Global Intifada', *The Washington Post* (16 February 1990).

7. For an analysis of this issue, see John L. Esposito and James P. Piscatori, 'Democratization and Islam', *The Middle East Journal*, ibid., 427–40.

8. For an analysis of the impact of the Islamic resurgence on non-Muslim communities, see John L. Esposito and Byron L. Haines, *The Impact of Islam*, *Pro Mundi Vita*, Bulletin 109 (1987/2).

9. Wafa Amr, 'Jordan Welcomes New Government, Political Freedoms', *Middle East Times* 9–15, 1990, 4.

Is Islam Threatened by Christianity?

Mohammed Arkoun

I hope that I may first be allowed to express my amazement that those responsible for this special issue of *Concilium* have chosen such a question. Why speak in terms of threat in connection with religions? Why not rather go into questions which are still pending, yet are decisive for a modern understanding of religion and all the great ideologies which have marked the history of societies and humanity generally? I am thinking, for example, of the need to shed more light on the relationship between violence, the sacred and the truth. We are aware of the extreme schematization of the 'holy war' – *jihād* – in the contemporary European imagination, with the constant portrayals of Islam and its warriors of Allah, going back to the Middle Ages. We are aware, too, how wars with a similar inspiration waged from the Christian side implicitly or explicitly receive some kind of legitimation when there is an emphasis on the intolerance, the fanaticism, the violence of Islam – 'the rage of Islam', to cite a recent expression used by B. Lewis.

But despite my hesitations about the approach chosen in this special issue, I am willing to discuss the question as put to me in the hope of guiding research and reflection towards more radical questions, which are more urgent for our time.

First I shall make some necessary comments on the terms Islam and Christianity; then I shall examine some basic facts which have sustained a potential threat posed by Christianity to Islam (and also vice versa) as shown in a number of historical situations; I shall end with a more direct response relating to the situation created since Vatican II.

I. Islam and Christianity

We all know that these two terms refer to vast heterogeneous complexes containing divisions and irreducible oppositions, despite the existence of a common 'symbolic capital', like revelation, the fundamental texts, a living tradition. On the basis of common facts which have become 'objective' for all believers, in the course of history distinct collective memories have been formed like Sunnism, Shi'ism and Kharijism in Islam; Orthodoxy, Catholicism and Protestantism in Christianity; and each of these great communities itself contains schools, groups – which the orthodox majorities call 'sects' – in greater or lesser numbers depending on the period.

These splits are not just sociological and political; they have theological foundations and consequences which, above all today, make it impossible to adopt the divisions imposed by the official literature of majority groups like Sunnism in Islam and the Catholic magisterium in the Middle Ages before Luther and Calvin. We need to respect this diversity, above all if we also recognize that these are the social agents in each historical situation which give changing expressions to each major historical trend of both Islam and Christianity.

Thus I do not see how Christianity, whether Orthodox, Catholic or Protestant, can threaten Indian, Indonesian or Turkish Islam. On the other hand, the missionary movement in Africa including the Maghreb was felt a threat by Muslims during the colonial period. It is in imitation of this that countries like Saudi Arabia or Libya have encouraged missionary activities, previously unknown under this form of Islam (except perhaps in the case of the Ismailis in the ninth and tenth centuries). I shall be returning to this aspect in the third part of this article.

Since Khomeini took power in Iran in February 1979, a very strong picture of Islam with a capital I has formed in the Western imagination (in Europe and North America). This is an artefact entirely constructed by the media, with the 'scientific' help of political literature which has not ceased to multiply reports, descriptions, 'analyses' of the 'fundamentalist' movements. It is no longer possible today to use the word Islam before a Western audience without immediately conjuring up powerful imagery combining the strongly negative connotations of the terms *jihād*, holy war, terrorism, fanaticism, violence, oppression of women, polygamy, repudiation, the veil as the Islamic headscarf, the rejection of the West, the violation of human rights, and so on.

I do not want to discuss here the relevance of these portrayals, which are in fact encouraged by the political talk of Muslims themselves who have been aiming over the last thirty years to legitimate their struggle in a variety of countries. It is worth remembering the mental obstacles erected in contemporary Western imagination over Islam, and in Muslim imagination over the 'West'. Here 'Islam' and 'West' have ceased to refer to their objective contents, whether religious, cultural, intellectual or historical; from now on they function as powerful conglomerates of images, of prejudices, of projections which call for two grids of mutual perception, two systems for legitimating all enterprises, exclusion and combat on both sides. The 'Westerners' make full use of these ideological conglomerates to justify the policy of controlling and rejecting Muslim immigrants; the 'Muslims' legitimate their struggle, even sacralizing it, by identifying imperialism, the missionary movement, Judaeo-Christianity as destructive wills which have been directed against the truth of Islam since its emergence. Here, certainly, the identification of Christianity with the West is even more systematic and more rigid than in the time of colonization. Later in this article, I shall try to demonstrate what we need to remember of these mental constructions which end up by setting up against each other not only two religions but two civilizations, even though they have common foundations, not to mention an axiology of common values.

II. Axiology of values and reciprocal exclusion

1. The reciprocal exclusion of systems

It is difficult to impose the notion of an axiology of common values on Judaism, Christianity and Islam. Either it suggests an unacceptable syncretism which appeals to the reference to one and the same God, the paradigm of the prophetic function, the teaching of the Ten Commandments; or the main emphasis is on the irreducible differences between the religion of love and the religions of a God who is distant, vengeful, inaccessible or even warlike. After the modern criticism of value, moreover, it is difficult to use such a concept with philosophers and social scientists.

However, believers in the three monotheistic religions continue to talk of God, revelation, prophets, sacred scriptures, spirituality, resurrection, eternal life, mysticism, prayer, pilgrimage, holiness, the sacred, moral values, and so on.

At the same time there is a reciprocal exclusion of theological, ethical, political systems constructed with the aid of the same mental equipment: the same vocabulary relating to homologous, if not identical representations. Exclusion was able to translate itself into wars like the Crusades, the Spanish Reconquista followed by the expulsion of the Jews and Muslims, or the struggles between the Ottoman Empire and Europe. It is in this same historical line that people today talk of the threat posed by

Islam to Europe and the West, which is identified with Christianity, set over against an 'Islam' seen as a homogenous grouping.

There is no denying that there is a latent violence in some people on both sides. In the Netherlands, passers-by watched indifferently the drowning of a small Moroccan girl; in Brittany one schoolboy killed another with a pistol; in Finland a Bangladeshi student was stabbed in the back with a knife ... . Islamic militants attack Western tourists, just as Hindus in India attack Muslims.

I do not think that it is fair to link this violent conduct with religion alone, although social psychology everywhere feeds on this simplistic 'explanation'. The media on both sides contribute towards reinforcing a religious imagery which, in the forms of integralism or fundamentalism, discredits Islam more than Christianity.

In the West, in fact, the academic establishment, the great names of research in social and political science, use their great power to drown the often timid secondary voices raised by Christianity (here, of course, I exclude the highly visible official interventions of John Paul II).

The exclusion in the West has moved from religious circles to university and scientific circles. Certainly not all of these circles; however, the dominant tendency, particularly among political scientists, is to demonstrate that 'Islam', presented as a homogeneous political force, threatens the basic values of the West, namely democracy, the constitutional state, human rights, the individual, the citizen, liberalism, the free market and the autonomy and sovereignty of reason which does away with the hypothesis of the existence of God, and so on.

The majority of Christian theologians, who have long resisted the philosophical postulates implicitly claimed as the foundations for the values in question,[1] have now been converted to what are regarded as the supreme achievements of Western thought. I am well aware that Christian morality continues to defend the spiritual vocation of the person; an ethic of responsibility for everything related to human beings; but one is also aware of the sarcastic comments of secular thinkers about the 'sermons' of another age.

The intellectual and psychological division within Western thought ceases to operate once 'the West' is confronted with Islam: then people slip into a consensus which on the one hand presupposes all the values listed above as achievements and on the other sees them rejected and menaced by fundamentalist barbarism (which might be called Communist or Socialist).

A prestigious American analyst, Samuel P. Huntington, recently published in the no less prestigious journal *Foreign Affairs* (72.3, 1992) a remarkable article entitled 'The Clash of Civilizations'. Here one can find a perfect illustration of the weight of the academic establishment which fashions 'scientifically', and thus in a reliable way, not only general opinion but also the vision of the great figures in foreign affairs.

2. Who is threatened? And who threatens?

What role does Christianity play in the different Western societies in which hegemony in all its forms – monetary, economic, political, intellectual, scientific, cultural – is trained to identify the dominant and the dominated, those who have the power to decide and act and those who react with derisory means, destructive but ineffective procedures, without ever achieving the historical stage of being societies like France, Great Britain, Germany – capable of forging their own destiny by working on themselves?

That raises the question of the historical responsibility of Christianity as the only religion connected, at least since the eighteenth century, with all the hegemonic enterprises of capitalist Europe and today in the West as incarnated in the 'Group of Seven'. I am not ignoring, once again, the 'ethical' protest of the churches, but I am stressing their intellectual solidarity with the authorities who produce and export contemporary 'scientific' knowledge at the same time as the philosophical postulates which relate to the destiny of the human condition. In the context of the Cold War people spoke of a Third World which still offered the strategic advantage of being a witness to the confrontation between the two great powers. Since intellectuals like Francis Fukuyama have proclaimed 'the end of history', there is only the liberal West on one side and the rest – or rather the residue – of the world on the other. So there is now no need to research the equivalent of an idea, a scientific, philosophical or theological position, in these societies which have been torn away from their memories, their cultural codes, their functional solidarities, and reduced within the space of thirty years to the state of residues of history, threatening by virtue of their demographic weight, open to being used as potential markets for the products of the great corporations, but long deprived of any capacity to contribute in a significant way to the model of action and thought imposed by the West.

The loud voice of John Paul II has the great merit of being omnipresent in the broken, divided, violent world which is forced to express its protests by transforming religious hope into fundamentalist rigidity and anti-human conduct. However, in the West itself, the intellectual and political elites are denouncing the dangers of a crusade of the great religions against the positive achievements of secularization: the freedoms of thought, of criticism, of creation, of transgressing the limits imposed by the dogmatic magisteria.

This controversy brings us back to oppositions known in the seventeenth and nineteenth centuries: Enlightenment reason affirming its sovereignty, its capacity to make the sole decision on good and evil, truth and falsehood, sense and nonsense; religious reason seeking to restore the servile judgment of a subject human spirit with recognition of the initiatives of God manifested in revelation (in its three modes: Jewish, Christian and Muslim).

The recurrence of the 'scholars' war' in France – note the violence of the expression currently used by the most influential protagonists – illustrates in a particularly instructive way the stagnation of thought in a crucial debate in a European society which has made a decisive contribution to the conquests of modernity. This same debate divides and tears apart Muslim societies with the same intensity, the same murderous intransigence, as that in revolutionary France between 1789 and 1795. Now neither Christian thought nor secular thought offer mental instruments, theories, ways of emancipation, spaces for research and communication which would allow the contemporaries involved in the dramas taking place in Muslim societies to by-pass the arguments, the oppositions, the divisions maintained in Western Christian contexts after at least four centuries of continuous confrontation. A critical examination of this situation seems to me a more urgent need and likely to be more productive in the present situation than fantasy questions about the threat that Islam and Christianity might pose to each other.

III. Towards a Vatican III

1. Why a Vatican III?

There is a great historic need to convene a Vatican III, which would go even further than Vatican II in integrating both the positive achievements in the sphere of critical thought and the political lessons learned from the development of the world since the 1960s.

It is as one who has been involved in the recent history of the Muslim countries, in particular those of the Maghreb, and as a historian of Islamic thought, that I would stress the urgent need for a Vatican III which would attempt to articulate a new language of hope, a semantic order which would be compelling for all consciences of the twentieth century, both those of the arrogant and cynical triumphalists who are everywhere, in both the West and the residuary societies, manipulating human passions and impotences, and those of the marginalized, the frustrated, the exploited, the dominated, the victims of uncontrolled forces.

This appeal for a Vatican III is in no way dictated by a theological privilege which would set Christianity above the other religious traditions: on the contrary, Vatican III would only be fulfilling a historical mission capable of giving hope to all men and women if it based its intervention on the explicit renunciation of all theological privilege, replacing it with a final recognition and integration of the plurality of human articulations of meaning.

As I have already indicated, Christianity in its Catholic and Protestant forms[2] is the only religion which, in what it has rejected and what it has accepted, has been continuously exposed to the challenges of a modernity which was forced and which developed in Europe and exclusively in Europe up until the Second World War. It is this historical position which confers on Christianity not so much an intrinsic superiority as an intellectual responsibility, which in my view also implies a moral and spiritual responsibility. To express my thought better, I would say that I am opposed to the secular position of Marcel Gauchet, which presents Christianity as 'the religion of the departure from the religious'[3] i.e. of a transition to a secularity promoted to the role of the insurpassable model which allows human beings to conceive of and construct their condition as historical beings. This is a lapse into a questionable specificity of Christianity and the exclusivism of a secular model which all too often nurtures so much arrogance in the West (see the Rushdie affair).

The problem posed by the resurgence of the religious in the form of combative ideologies and refuges for identity is not so much that of knowing how definitively to depart from religions as how to cope with the situational tasks to which we are tied by a procedural, instrumental reason which also manages to make us forget or delay the work which is most urgent and most vital for all societies, that of the re-establishment, the reappropriation, the universalization of the meaning of human existence and action, the existence and action of *all* human beings and not just those whom various chances have led to be born in the privileged places of the hegemonical world.

Even if it were to meet in the near future, Vatican III would not by itself be able to set in motion such an orientation of all contemporary societies. But it would have cultural, intellectual and institutional resources, the moral credit, the channels of transmission and the historical and symbolic capital which are required today in any intervention on behalf of humanity, its most effective protection, promotion and liberation in the course of the twentieth century.

I shall now venture to go further in developing this utopia by setting out the main lines of reflection that would need to be followed and the programme for action that would have to be proposed to the world.

2. Lines of reflection and a programme of action

(a) How do we move from the era of inter-religious dialogue encouraged by Vatican II to the era of a thought and action founded on the historical solidarity and integration of the peoples? This solidarity would aim to put an end to the ideological connivance of states which conclude agreements to 'co-operate' to the detriment of those peoples who do not have state representatives. The quest for *official* spokesmen eliminating independent personalities has been pursued by the churches since the 1960s with the same constancy as that to be found among democratic states. In politics and economics, as in inter-religious dialogue, the results have been negative and sometimes even scandalous.

(b) How do we move from theologies founded on themselves, with an exclusively communitarian aim, to a radical criticism, without concessions to religious reason as it has functioned and continues to function in all known religious traditions? We know how far these theologies, particularly in the religions 'of revelation' or 'the Book', have functioned up till now as cultural systems of reciprocal exclusion, an exclusion which recurs in the course of the political confrontations and expansionist strategies in the Mediterranean area from the emergence of Islam on.[4]

(c) How do we surmount the psychological, cultural and philosophical division between religious reason and Enlightenment reason that thinkers like Kant, Hegel, Durkheim and Max Weber have reinforced rather than transcended? On 12 December 1989, the bicentenary year of the French Revolution, Cardinal Lustiger refused to take part in the opening Republican Ceremony led by Abbé Grégoire at the Pantheon. Thus two centuries after the event, the theological and philosophical confrontation between revelation and revolution had made hardly any progress.

What could Vatican II do to open new horizons of thought and action not only for the Christian/secularized societies of the West, but for all the cultural traditions which are in the process of facing the same challenges as a universal category of human history? For the study of the relations between revelation and revolution has not been exhausted.

(d) When one sees how Rome continues to suspend from teaching theologians judged to be deviant, one can only dare to hope that Vatican III will consent to opening institutions of teaching and research to true comparative study of religion. I was able to make an extended survey in the universities of Europe and America of the teaching of religious history and anthropology; my findings were that most often the study of Islam is relegated to Departments of Oriental Studies; when there is a chair for Islam in an institute for the history of religions, teaching is twisted round so that it becomes a juxtaposition of various kinds of factual knowledge, i.e. a description of an ethnographic kind which neglects any comparative and anthropological approach.

One might add that the teaching of religions is dominated either by a concern for orthodoxy and edification in establishments controlled by the religious authorities or by the agnostic indifference and cold erudition of the state universities. Certainly there are people who are aware of the issues that I am attempting to define here, but they are not managing to change a general situation marked by the imbalance between the knowledge that is being developed and the pressing demands which are multiplying in all societies.

3. Responses

It is impossible to present here an exhaustive list of all the areas that Vatican III could open up, the hopes that it could regenerate, the solutions it could propose. But why not, someone might say, impose the same responsibilities on Judaism, Islam, Hinduism and Buddhism? Is it not inconsistent to favour a Vatican III in this way, when Christianity continues to be denounced for its evident solidarity with the power-plays of the West?

I have two answers to these questions. The first is that Vatican III must finish off the work begun by Vatican II in developing in rich societies the idea of a welcoming, effective, coherent democracy for all men and women. The second is that Christianity is benefitting from a historical position which at present the other religions cannot attain: it expresses itself, it acts, it develops in societies which have attained a level of democratization, of the conquest and diffusion of knowledge, material wealth, scientific and technological possibilities the equivalent of which is still far out of reach of the rest of the world. If despite all these advantages Christianity imprisons itself, like the democracies themselves, in a sole concern to preserve its achievements and protect them against barbarian invasions, then the whole of Western civilization will give way to other beginnings. That is, unless the secular forces which contributed to producing it bring about an intellectual and spiritual revolution comparable in its impact on the world to that of 1789 in France. Then it will be the religious dimension of history which reveals its impotence to improve human existence and its structural links with outdated phases of cultures and civilizations.

This call for a Vatican III contains an implicit refutation of all discourse which presents Islam as a growing threat to the values of the West. The majority Muslim opinion is impervious to the idea of a critical survey of the intellectual, religious and political history of Islam. Broad and powerful social strata are expressing the problems of life, are legitimately rebelling against the incompetence, not to mention the treason of the political, economic and cultural 'élites', very quickly converted into parasite classes after the euphoria of the regaining of independence in the 1950s and 1960s. The social and political tensions, the pressures of an unfavourable international environment, do not leave room for efforts at rehabilitating Islam or making it capable of playing a historical role which is intellectually and spiritually compelling for modern consciences. It is precisely this dramatic historical situation which neither a West concerned for power, comfort and productivity nor a Christianity hardly relieved of its missionary dogma want to take charge of, though both have contributed to its genesis since the nineteenth century.

I am aware of all the utopian aspects of my call for a Vatican III. I wanted at least to show how a Muslim intellectual is now trying to speak of a Christianity which could make all the tragic confrontations with Islam since the Crusades a thing of the past. I hope that utopia will serve to indicate the distance which today lies between Christianity and the hegemonical West and their historical responsibility.

Translated by John Bowden

Notes

1. I recall that the Catholic church only signed the United Nations Declaration on Human Rights under John XXIII, an indication of a theological resistance to philosophical postulates which were judged unacceptable given the religious status of a person as distinct from the person as individual and citizen.

2. I reserve for examination elsewhere the case of Orthodox Christianity, which since Byzantium has been linked to what Western Europe, a place of mental, cultural and institutional schisms, has called the 'East'. The seventy years of Communist persecution have contributed to complicating the present situation of Orthodox Christianity.

3. Cf. M. Gauchet, *Le desenchantement du monde*, Paris.

4. Cf. the classic work by Henri Pirenne, *Mahomet et Charlemagne*, and Norman Daniel, *Islam and the West*, Oxford 1993.

III · Challenges

Tawhīd: The Recognition of the One in Islam

V. J. Cornell

I. One, unique and transcendent

In Morocco, a story is sometimes told in the circles of Sufīs (Muslim mystics) in which a spiritual master from the countryside went unrecognized for years because, as a child, he had the reputation of being a stubborn and uncomprehending student. This was especially true in mathematics, where the boy could never seem to pass beyond the first level. To the great consternation of his teacher, he would always give the same answer to every problem: What is 2+2? 'One.' What is 2−2? 'One.' What is 35 × 144? 'One.' What is the square root of 16? 'One.'

The moral of this anecdote recalls the one-hundred-and-twelfth *sūra*, or discourse, of the Qur'ān. The four 'signs' (*āyāt*) or verses of this discourse are widely understood by Muslims to provide the paradigmatic definition of *tawhīd*, a concept usually defined as unicity, or the oneness of God:

> Say: He is Allāh, the Only,
> Allāh the Perfect, beyond compare.
> He gives not birth, nor is He begotten,
> And He is, in Himself, not dependent on anything.[1]

Tawhīd – specifically, the belief that God is one, unique, and transcendent – constitutes the fundamental theological premise of Islam. Because the Arabic word *islām* connotes surrender, submission and giving oneself up to another's disposal, *tawhīd* also implies that universal *islām* – submission to God as the sole Master of destiny and ultimate Reality – is an ontological state that pertains to all of creation. Since human beings, unlike animals and angels, are endowed with the capacity of choice, it is both a mercy and a challenge from God that humankind's realization of *tawhīd* has to be voluntarily confirmed. The first step toward salvation in Islam is thus the conscious submission of one's individual will to That which manifestly *is*. It is only at this stage of spiritual understanding that a person can truly be called a *muslim*, or 'one who submits to God'. Each Muslim must reaffirm *tawḥīd* every day, through inward remembrance as well as outward prayer, even if he is born into a nominally 'Muslim' family. For reasons such as these, classical Muslim theologians saw acceptance of the historical religion revealed by God through the Prophet Muḥammad (*al-dīn al-Muhammadī*) – the 'Islam' of world history – as the most natural and logical product of human intellection.

II. Pre-Islamic beliefs and the Qur'an

In the language of modern theology, *tawḥīd* includes both monotheism and monism. As monotheism, it is absolute, radical and uncompromising. The socio-religious environment of Pre-Islamic Arabia, the context in which Islam arose, exhibited much of the doctrinal eclecticism character- istic of the fringes of the Late Antique world. Mecca, the birthplace of the Prophet Muḥammad and site of the initial Qur'ānic revelations, was a regional commercial centre whose economic livelihood was legitimized by an accretive cult that unsystematically assimilated a wide variety of beliefs and traditions. The Abrahamic tradition was present in the myth of the Ka'ba ('Cube') – the symbolic centre of Meccan pilgrimage – which was believed to have been a temple consecrated to Allāh ('The God', *ho theos*) by Abraham and his son Ishmael, the 'fathers' of the Arab people. This paramount deity, even in the pre-Islamic period, was characterized by transcendence. His abode was the heavens, and no image was ever made of him. Fertility cults were connected with Mecca as well, as evidenced by the association of the site with Hagar (the mother of Ishmael), the nurturing spring of Zamzam, and the fact that the pagan pilgrimage involved circumambulation of the Ka'ba by women clad only in a leather breech-cloth. Modern scholars have also discerned in the pre-Islamic cult traces of Hermetism, Zurvanism (the veneration of time as an entity), animism and totemism. Mediating figures included Hellenistic goddesses ('daughters' of Allah), angels, immortals (whether Iranian or Hermetic is unclear), *jinn* ('inspiring' spirits similar to the Roman *genii*), and even biblical prophets.

The Qur'ānic revelation swept away this colourful Babel with a compelling call to belief in Allāh (the supreme God in any case) as the one and only divinity. In Qur'ānic discourse, Allāh is, before everything, the merciful creator and sustainer of all that exists. In theological terms, his most important attributes are *unity and simplicity*:

He is Allah, there is no other god but He; Knower of the unseen and the seen, He is the Merciful, the Compassionate.

He is Allah, there is no other god but He; Possessor of All, the Holy, the Source of Security, the Keeper of Faith, the Vigilant, the Glorious, the Irresistible, the Most Supreme; Exalted is He beyond what [the pagans] associate with Him (LIX [al-Ḥashr], 22–23).

Allāh in the Qur'ān thus encompasses all of the attributes of divinity previously ascribed to lesser gods in pre-Islamic religion. This divinity *in extenso* is expressed through reference to the ninety-nine 'beautiful names' of God (7 [al-A'rāf, 180), of which some are mentioned in the verses given above. Allāh is no longer just a powerful but distant creator who leaves earthly details to lesser beings. As master (*Mawlā*) of the universe, God actively involves himself in all aspects of his dominion at every moment in time. He is also more than the first principle of Hellenistic philosophers or an abstract law of existence, such as *Rta* in the Indian Rig Veda. Allāh is a personally accessible master who hears and responds to the needs of his slave ('abd): 'I am indeed close; I answer the prayer of the supplicant when he calls on Me' (II [al-Baqara], 186).

Unlike the God of Judaism or Christianity, Allāh is also beyond either ethnic association or gender. Allāh in Islam is never known as 'the God of our fathers', because each Muslim community, whatever its race or origin, constitutes an equally valid 'kingdom of priests and a holy nation' (Exodus, 19.4–6). Nor is Allāh referred to as 'Our Father, who art in heaven', because, as a truly transcendent deity, he must transcend gender as well. The God of Islam encompasses both traditionally 'male' attributes such as those of generation and domination and 'female' attributes, such as those of loving-kindness and nurturance. Allāh is called 'He' only because of the nature of the Arabic language, which assigns male or female to all nouns and pronouns. Indeed, it is probably not coincidental that so much mystical poetry in Islam has been written in Persian, a language with no gender markers to convey unintended theological limitations.

The perspectives of both monism and monotheism can be found in the Qur'ānic passage, 'He is the First and the Last, the Outward and the Inward; And He is the Knower of every thing' (LVII [al-Ḥadīd], 3). From the point of view of 'monism', this means that the object of a person's submission is always one, whether or not he is aware of it: 'To God belong the east and the west. Wheresoever you may turn, there is the face of God' (II [al-Baqara], 115). From the perspective of monotheism, however, the statement means that God is an omniscient, unitary totality that is beyond all description or allusion. This perspective of absolute transcendence, known in Islamic theology as *tanzīh*, has profound implications for one's understanding of both divinity and human salvation. In the first place, verses such as that given above serve as 'signs' which signify that God is not only paramount, but Absolute. This fact, as we have already seen, is the fundamental premise of Islam. Acknowledgment of this premise by the human intellect – which amounts to recognition of the truth of ontological *islām* – initiates a logical series of derivative conclusions, mediated by the 'signs' of the Qur'ān and divine grace, that drastically reconfigures the Muslim's world-view. One is now able to understand that the starting-point for all human vanity is to imagine that God-as-Absolute is something other than what He clearly *is*. To assert that there is more than one absolute or that the relative is absolute is both the height of folly and the source of disbelief. This awareness of the unitary truth of God, to the earliest companions of the Prophet Muḥammad as well as to later theologians, was deemed so important as to constitute the essence of knowledge itself. On comparing this revolutionary realization with the attitudes that they formerly held in the past, the first generation of Muslims could only see themselves as having lived in a state of all-encompassing ignorance, or *jāhiliyya*.

III. Islamic criticism of christology

For Islam, then, as for all 'Abrahamic' faiths, it is the truth that makes one free. On a certain level of abstraction, this truth is identical for Christianity, Judaism and Islam alike – the ultimate reality of the one God, profound in his uniqueness and simplicity. From another perspective, however, the Christian version of monotheism is different enough from the Muslim and Jewish models to pose a serious contradiction. For Christianity, the human being is born into a world of carnality. Being unable, because of his worldly nature, to comprehend his true deiformity, carnal man is in need of a saving miracle to shock him back into consciousness. This salvific shock is provided through the historical advent of Christ, who miraculously manifested the two polarities of the human condition (the deiform and the worldly) in a single person. Christ, in his mercy, allowed the hypostatic unfolding of this miracle to continue throughout time, so that salvation may be attained in the post-Christic age. As a final gift, he also bore mankind's sins as a sacrifice so that all humanity – despite their absorption in the flesh – may be forgiven.

The trouble with this model from the Muslim point of view is its inherent illogicality. Aristotle's principle of non-contradiction (a maxim accepted by both Christian and Muslim theologians) states that a proposition cannot be both true and false in regard to the same thing at the same time. From this standpoint, it is impossible for Christ to have been purely man and purely God in a single manifestation. This may have been a reason why Muslim legists in the caliphal age favoured the supposed duophysitism of the Nestorian church over other Christian doctrines. A more important problem, however, was that this same principle of non-contradiction implied that a truly transcendent God can never become incarnate in a human body. This, in fact, is the perspective of the Qur'ān, which categorically states: 'He gives not birth, nor is He begotten.' Even the 'mystery' of the Trinity is insufficient for resolving this theological difficulty: 'They deny the Truth who say: "Allāh is one of three," for there is no god but Allāh' (V [al-Mā'ida], 73).

One of the most powerful theological arguments in favour of Islamic *tawhīd* is that the *muwahhid*, or believer in the oneness of God, does not have to resort to an abandonment of logic to maintain his faith. While the Qur'ān implicitly accepts the idea of God's immanence (*tashbīh*) in the world, the normative force of the Islamic doctrine of transcendence makes it impossible to conceive of Jesus (or Muhammad, or any other prophet for that matter) as more than a mortal being.

Indeed, while acknowledging the importance of Jesus as the last prophet of Israel, the Qur'ān explains the miracle of his birth as being analogous to the creation of Adam: 'Verily, the similitude of Jesus before God is that of Adam; He created him from earth, and then said to him: "Be!" and he was' (III [Al'Imrān], 59). Such an assertion is in full agreement with the principle of non-contradiction. After all, if humanity itself was created by the 'miracle' of God's blowing life into clay, is it any more miraculous for God to infuse the same spirit into the womb of Mary?

As for the Trinity, although certain Sufis and Muslim philosophers acknowledged the relevance of the classical *logos endiathetos* (immanent word), *logos spermatikos* (seminal word), and *logos prophorikos* (expressed word) as explanations for Divine immanence, such doctrines were considered too intellectual for the ordinary believer. In foolish or deceitful hands, the idea that the divine is somehow present in man could easily be distorted to mean that man himself can become God.

In another sense, however, it is possible to dispense altogether with theological arguments over the historical and metahistorical hypostases of Christ. This is because the salvation perspective of Islam, founded as it is on the capacity of the human being to acknowledge the reality of *tawhīd*, makes the salvific nature of Christ unnecessary. In Islam, man is not viewed as a lost creature who needs a miracle to save him from perdition. Just before their emergence into creation, the descendants of Adam 'cut' the covenant that compels the human race to acknowledge their Lord and Creator: 'Then your Lord drew forth the progeny of the children of Adam from their marrow. And He made them testify concerning themselves, [saying]: "Am I not your Lord" "Surely, we so testify!"' (7 [al-A'rāf], 172).

Knowledge of a transcendent God requires transcendent intelligence – or at least an intellect capable of conceiving of the Absolute. If, as Muslim tradition claims, God created the world in order to be known, it is necessary that human beings be given the capacity to recognize and understand the Truth that brought about their existence. When the Qur'ān exhorts the thinking person to look up from the 'signs' of God between its pages and see the signs that testify to his reality in the world, it is not engaging in mere sophistry. Despite his existence in the world, man's 'Adamic' nature have already equipped him with the intellect and common sense to lead him towards salvation. The *qur'ān* – the 'reading' which never ceases – came down from Allāh as a mercy for humankind, and its repetition in the hearts of the faithful and on the written page continually informs the human being that he can save himself.

Notes

1. Translations of Qur'ānic passages are by the present author and include definitions based on an etymological analysis of Arabic roots and the consensus of the Islamic exegetical tradition.

The Challenge of Islamic Monotheism: A Christian View

Adolfo González Montes

I. The controversy inherited from the past

Relations between Muslims and Christians have a long history of hostilities and antagonisms of all kinds. Without embarking on an analysis of the historical, social and political factors involved in these relationships, though keeping them clearly in mind to avoid being trapped in pure abstraction, I shall attempt to explore some ideas about the way in which the Islamic concept of God influences Islamic-Christian religious dialogue. This influence is so strong that the theological difference underlying it has prevented many European nations bordering the Islamic peoples from overcoming cultural, and to some extent political, distance, despite a common history, emotional ties and common interests created by that proximity, ties that have been reinforced in the present by mutual economic dependence.

It is impossible to evade the fact that this proximity has been replaced in some cases during recent decades by forced association, since the massive immigration of Muslims into the European countries has affected the social, cultural and religious texture of these Christian countries. The historical past continues to weigh heavily and, although it is true that the ancient Christian societies of Europe are now heavily secularized, the Christian inspiration of their histories has made them incompatible with Islam. The European nations have seen Muslim expansion as a real threat to their faith and independence as free peoples inspired by Christianity. Is it still possible today to maintain this distance that continues to keep the two apart culturally through its historic religious inspiration? Are there not in fact theological reasons for closer relations between Muslims and Christians?

The historical controversy between the two religions is centred theologically on the concept of God. The controversy here has had three stages, from the Christian point of view, which Rizzardi defines as follows: 1. Islam is regarded as a christological and trinitarian heresy (11th–15th centuries); 2. Islam is treated as a separate religion (16th–19th centuries); 3. Islam is included in the universal economy of salvation (20th century).[1] The process is an evolution in theological judgment that starts from the need to eliminate 'difference' and moves finally to integration in a theological paradigm of revelation capable of including both religions. While there are scholars who accuse the Latin controversialists of a fundamental error in attributing to Islam a theology and christology in competition with those of Christianity, such a view has probably only very general validity, since many of these controversialists regarded Islam as not so much a heresy but as a general residue of errors.[2]

Consequently, apart from demonstrating the heretical nature of Islam, the controversialists were not concerned with the place of Islam within the Christian economy, but its relationship with it.[3] The Latin scholars were aware that Islam's challenge to Christianity stems from its rejection of the trinitarian concept of God. They attributed Islam's opposition to this to what they regarded as Muhammad's 'false prophecy', nourished by heretical Christian communities and sects with which he had contact, and were implacable in this view. However, apart from the hermeneutical problem, the Latin anti-Islamic controversy offers a basis for a preliminary conclusion: the Latins saw and experienced Islam as a threat to faith in the God of Jesus Christ and felt that this threat had a particular christological focus that made it completely impossible to come to terms with the Qur'an's theology of Jesus.[4]

II. The centre of the controversy: 'theological difference'

What then is the theological difference that, even if we modify the starting point of the Islamic controversialists, leads Christians to feel that Islamic monotheism is a threat to their own faith? To say that Islamic monotheism is anti-trinitarian is insufficient, even given that this implies the rejection of Christ's divinity. This is in fact the result of something prior, something that is the real basis of this rejection of Christian christology. What is prior is the idea of God implied by the revelatory mission of Muhammad, which makes plain the theological nature of this monotheism as something imcompatible with two

Christian concepts implicit in the notion of revelation, incarnation and redemption. So intrinsic is redemption to the Christian concept of revelation that, although the idea of revelation is more general than that of salvation, Christianity, like Judaism, sees divine revelation as mediated in the history of human salvation. When Christian theology set itself the task of reformulating the scholastic premises of faith in dialogue with modern schools of philosophy, it was forced to face (in theologies ranging from Rahner to Gutiérrez and Segundo in the theology of liberation) a concept of revelation totally inclusive of the various elements in the history of religion (I do not wish to discuss here the legitimacy of this venture), but above all including its own character as a history of salvation. Rahner raised not only the question of the relationship of general history to the particular *historia salutis* (Israel-Christ-the church), but also that of its own saving character. The Reformation diluted theology into soteriology when it thought it saw a threat to Christian theological discourse from 'natural theology', but *Cur Deus homo?* is, in essence, part of the core of all Christian theologizing. Alongside the models of answers devised by theology to Anselm's question since the twelfth century, before Anselm put the question into circulation the pre-Nicene Fathers had begun to answer it by making the shift from *oikonomia* to *theologia* by equating the *sermo de Christo* with the *sermo de Deus*.

Any Christian theologian accepts that the concept of redemption receives its specific content from the incarnation, the key to Chalcedonian christology (thought not vice versa). And it is at this point that the two concepts, the one including the other, make Christianity alien to Muslim monotheism. However, it cannot be said that to accept any idea of incarnation would be completely incompatible with the Islamic concept of revelation, if by incarnation is understood the instantiation within history of divine revelation. From this point of view, if the Qur'an represents a challenge to the Christian tendency – always heretical, but real, if only through naivety – to slip into tritheism or idolatry and assimilate God to the world, should Islam not also consider the fact of the instantiation in the world of the divine Word in the book of the Qur'an? Could it do this in a way that brought it close to the Christian idea of the incarnation of the Word of God?

The erroneous idea that Christianity and Judaism, with Islam, are the three 'religions of the book', branches springing from a common Abrahamic trunk, is based on the conviction that the medium that makes the divine revelation public in the three is a sacred book. With the knowledge we have today of the Jewish religion, and on the basis of textual and literary criticism of the Old Testament, it is clear that only the rabbinic theology of the Law developed anything that could be called a theology of revelation through a book. This theology was attacked by Paul in the polemic in which he contrasted the revelation of the mystery of God in Jesus Christ with the mediation of revelation in the Law. Only a few schools deriving from the Reformation came close to anything like the religion of the book. Strictly speaking, only Islam is a religion of the book in that the worldly and historical shape of revelation is embodied in the Qur'an as the book that has been revealed in a way that is not comparable with the Bible and the New Testament, which are sacred texts in so far as they bear witness to the incarnation of the Word, but are in no sense identical with the incarnation in their objective material, written or phonetic, form.

There is no getting away from the decisive effect on Protestantism of the Enlightenment critique of the identification of scripture with the Word of God. The identity of both is based on the historical occurrence of revelation as a 'language event' that takes place first in the prophetic proclamation and, 'in the fullness of time', in the unveiling in history of the identity of the Son with the Father, to prolong his work of revelation and salvation in the preaching of the church and the sacraments. Throughout this event the written expression of the revelation experience is a means of God's self-communication, but this always transcends the expression. Although the Qur'an is the objective revelation of the divine Word, the experience of revelation is different in Christianity, which has no knowledge of the book pre-existing in final written form in God, as Islam describes the Qur'an, but knows the divine Word, which took to itself the humanity of Jesus in the historical event. In this sense the incarnation is greater than the mere expression within the world of the divine will in something that, by remaining unchanged, maintains its identity as the atemporal expression of an absolute divine Law.

The incarnation of God in Christ is a salvation event that identifies itself with the event of life through God's identifying with life from within its course. Only God's love makes it possible to understand something like this, by revealing to human beings the ultimate purpose of the divine self-abasement, namely to rescue sinful human beings from their slide towards death. God's aseity in the Qur'an makes him ontologically distant from the realities of the world. In affirming this uniqueness of God, the Qur'an seeks to avoid the danger of idolatry that is inherent in the Christian tendency to tritheism, which is an error always possible, even if formally tritheism is a heresy. In other words, the Qur'an's concern is directly opposed both to polytheism and to an idolatrous involvement of God with the world (4, 171).[5] From this point of view Islamic monotheism challenges Christianity by arousing in Christian sensibilities the same repugnance at a confusion between God and the world that could lead to replacing God by human beings and their own works and constructs. Even if Christians accept the challenge, however, they will always find that their faith reaches an unsurmountable barrier in Islam's rejection of Chalcedonian christology.

Some theologians have proposed a theology of the Trinity as the basis for the situation of human nature as involved in discourse – that is, questioned and questioning[6] – and dialogue, which also excludes the totalitarianism of political monotheism as violating democratic freedoms.[7] It is precisely the incarnation of the Word and the action of the Spirit in history that provide a theological channel for religious and cultural plurality, without thereby abandoning the trinitarian ontology that underpins them. The danger of these proposals, however, is that of identifying God either with the exhausted past (Jüngel) or with historical process (Moltmann) without the necessary *diastasis* between God and the world. Islamic monotheism will certainly contribute to highlighting more starkly the limitations of a theology of the Trinity that assimilates the cross of Christ to the historical pain of the world, since the identification of God with the world cannot affect God's transcendence over the world. It is from this point of view that Islam sees the Christian tradition of the resurrection and ascension of Jesus Christ as the ultimate triumph of God over the enemies of the 'Word and Spirit of God', the prophet Jesus (4.157–8). Christianity's stress on the identity of God and God's world in the incarnation and *kenosis* of the Word makes it difficult to overcome the temptation to a sort of theopathy incompatible with divine transcendence, which is not the same as eliminating from the concept of God the dynamism of the intra-Trinitarian love that goes out beyond itself and manifests itself in the love story of the 'Son of God'.

III. Is it impossible to harmonize both religions in relation to salvation history?

It does seem that theological difference makes it impossible to link Islam and Christianity in relation to the universal divine plan, because the relativization of Christ by Muhammad represents not only the integration of Christ into an inclusive universal economy of prophetic revelation, but also ultimate opposition to the history of Christ as the history of God by virtue of the idea of *tawhīd* or the oneness of God.[8] Nevertheless, Islamic christology can form an important corrective to the Christian tendency to misinterpret the consubstantiality of the Son with the Father, and identify Christ with the Father, without falling into an inter-trinitarian 'difference' between the two based on Christ's condition of Logos and eternal Son and as such, 'God incarnate'. Nevertheless, maintaining this difference within the Godhead does not meet Islam's requirements. Conversely, Christianity's attempt to move closer to Islam, in its concern to make the necessary stress on the 'difference' between the Father and the Son, for its part involves the risk of tipping Christian christology towards modern forms of adoptionism based on Islamic christology, supported by the rationalism of contemporary thought. All of which goes to show that the attempt to reconcile both religions under a single schema of divine revelation, albeit not for the moment a soteriological model, is far from easy. Each presents itself with a clear desire for absoluteness and seeks to be the ultimate arbiter of God's revelation.

(*a*) Modern Christian theology of religion – very remote from the Barthian paradigm that regarded revelation as the 'abolition of religion' – has made it possible to reconsider some core doctrinal concepts of the pre-Nicene (Justin, Alexandrian) theology of the Logos to explain the trinitarian basis of the presence of the Word in the historical development of religions by incorporating them into an economy of revelation that sees Christ as the ultimate manifestation of God. This theology is based on the incarnation of the divine Word as the substratum of the gradual historical development of religious awareness. This makes it possible to incorporate into the Christian economy the contribution of other religions to revelation and salvation, according to *Nostra Aetate* (2). This theology in no way presupposes the assimilation of Christ to the history of the prophets in isolation from his divine state, which is the basis for the ultimate claims of the New Testament revelation: the divinity of Jesus Christ embodies the theological principle that explains the significance of the abrogation of the Mosaic Law and the relativization of any other religious sensibility.

(*b*) Behind Islamic opposition to Christian christology is the desire to defend a totally comprehensive monotheism, which is theological, not cultural, in nature but which also has clear political implications, which inspire some of the current forms of Islamic fundamentalism. Christianity too has historically had this tendency, but the 'evangelical principle' of

Christianity has prevented it from being transposed into politics as a religious system. Being theological, Islam's 'political principle' finds its best explicitation in opposition to Christian christology. Islam seeks the definitive overthrow of Christianity as an economy of revelation by incorporating Jesus into the history of prophetic revelation, because what Islam knows about Jesus is not in fact christology but theology. Jesus is the word of God (*kalimat Allāh*), and was given the Spirit, not to be a manifestation of God and his mystery, but to be at his service and declare his unalterable will, the goal of which is the total submission of human beings to the divine will, the object of the prophecy that culminates in the Koran.[9] It is true that Jesus too reveals the sovereign will of God in his obedience, but the presence of God in his person makes that the very revelation of God as redemptive love. This is completely foreign to Islam.

Islam's monotheism originally sought to overcome the tribal differences in the Arab world, and at the same time to unite all peoples under the sovereignty of Allah. It could be said that in its universalism it mirrors Christianity and therefore its conflict with it is direct, but in Christianity it is precisely the theology of the incarnation and paschal mystery of Christ, because it is based on the divine state of the one who 'abases' himself and takes on the human state (Phil. 2), that makes it possible to distinguish between the reign of God – which is hidden, and does not allow us to know, except by faith, where God's victory has been won – and the reign of this world, and also between the church and secular political organization.

Some of the misunderstandings of the past derive from the un-founded belief that Islam was reacting to a mistaken interpretation of Christian christology. Although in its beginnings the rejection of the divine Trinity was based on wrong information about it, as when the Qur'an seems to think that the divine Trinity is Allah, Jesus and Mary (5.116), Islam is nonetheless very clear that its own goal is to relativize Christian christology. Islamic monotheism regards divine sovereignty as safeguarded only by the ultimacy of Muhammad's mission, the seal of prophecy. This implies the incorporation of Christ into prophecy, and the removal of his divinity, with the consequent neutralization of the theological principle of Christian christology. It can be said that this theology was formulated in a Hellenistic mode,[10] but even so, and apart from the formulations, the issue Christian faith raises remains in its core and intention irreducible to the Islamic view, unless it abandons (and this is not just a matter of hermeneutics) the affirmation of what the church sought to preserve by using the resources of Hellenistic philosophy, which was in any case perfectly comprehensible to the Islamic scholastic tradition.

I find myself forced to admit to a deep perplexity at the difficulty and believe that the continuation of theological dialogue is essential. Not only must Christianity strive to understand the categories of Islamic theology of revelation, but Islam too must pay closer attention to the central category of Christian theology, that is, the incarnation of the divine Word, because it has resources to understand it, though Christianity would regard them as inadequate. In the meantime, however, I regard the defence of the religious freedom of all, and its permanent entrenchment through the democratic ordering of society, as the essential framework for co-operation. Attempts to formulate christology in language closer to Islamic thought cannot mean an abandonment of the Christian dogma of the Trinity, which is an example within the Godhead of a dialogue-based understanding of human existence free of all totalitarianism. The weakness of faith in the Crucified Lord is something else that is different from the weakness of a Christianity that increasingly erodes its own understanding of faith.

Translated by Francis McDonagh

Notes

1. G. Rizzardi, *La sfida dell' islam*, Milan 1992, 30.
2. The mediaevalist Norman Daniel believes that even Peter of Cluny (the Venerable) regarded Islam as a heretical position that included all the anti-trinitarian heresies (*Islam and the West*, Edinburgh 1960). Rizzardi also cites the texts of Peter the Venerable's *Summa totius haeresis saracenorum* (*La sfida dell' Islam*, 30), but believes that these texts prove that for Peter of Cluny Muhammad was not so much a Christian heretic in the technical sense ('heresy goes out from the church and turns against the church') as a pseudo-prophet, and his insistence on calling Islam a heresy is based on his acceptance of the Augustinian definition of heresy (cf. Rizzardi, 36–7).
3. Rizzardi, *La sfida dell' islam* (n. 1), 38–9.
4. Cf. R. Arnaldez, *Jésus, fils de Marie, prophète de l'Islam*, Paris 1980.
5. Rizzardi, *La sfida dell' islam* (n. 1), 271.
6. E. Jüngel, *God as the Mystery of the World*, Edinburgh and Grand Rapids, MI, 1983.
7. J. Moltmann, *The Trinity and the Kingdom of God*, London and New York 1982, 191–222.
8. 'The idea of *tawhīd*, the oneness of God, is extremely rich, and later dogmatic developments interpret it in the most rigoristic possible fashion,' E. M. Pareja, *La religiosidad musulmana*, Madrid 1975, 25.

9. Cf. R. Arnaldez, *Jésus dans la pensée musulmane*, Paris, 1988, 14ff.

10. H. Küng, 'Towards an Ecumenical Theology of Religions: Some Theses for Clarification', *Concilium* 183, 1986, 119–25.

Human Rights in Islam

Mahmud Gamal-ad-din

I. The International Charter of Human Rights – A European Formulation

The topic of human rights and its international or – to make the topic more precise – global significance cannot be discussed unless we first consider the great spiritual and cultural diversity of peoples.

1. The European historical background

The phenomenon of 'human rights' is the product of a variety of factors. The spirit and culture of the Western world generally have stamped notions of human rights in recent times. So many people have believed that this is something new for the Islamic public, though in Islamic under-standing the expression 'human rights' could simply denote a re-formulation of traditional rights. That the spirit and culture of the West have so far dominated the question of human rights can be explained from the way in which the idea of human rights, its dissemination and implementation in the West, derives from Western thinkers and philosophers. In particular, the injustices suffered by the European population before and at the beginning of the Renaissance left their mark on European thought. They supported the hypothesis that law created by international conventions is always also exposed to the misuse of power. The Declaration of Human Rights therefore gave the impression that the rights which are obtained for men and women primarily protect them from the interference of state powers. It is indisputable that there are plausible reasons for this European view. Indeed, the more that traditional human rights increased, the more the influence of secular and religious authorities shrank and relaxed its pressure on citizens.

In reality, this view of things by no means applies to all the societies of the world. It is completely alien to some Far Eastern countries (e.g.

Japan). Japan did not experience the explosive and fundamental conflict between citizens and nobility which was typical for Europe. The same is true of the Islamic countries, in particular those countries which until most recently were subjected to European imperialism. Their problem was not the authorities in their own country but foreign colonial rule, from which they had to be freed because it represented aggression not only against their territorial sovereignty but also against the totality of their own law, culture, tradition and public good.

2. *European conceptuality*

Furthermore, in international treaties the definition and conceptual interpretation of human rights largely draws on a European intellectual attitude, in connection both with their validity for individuals and the rights of the community. There is no doubt that the European view of human rights attaches too much significance to political and social freedom, which is not always kept in balance. Furthermore the individual citizen is unacceptably accorded too much (individual) freedom in the exercising of his or her political rights. This does damage to the rights of the community and also to behaviour on the part of the individual member of society which is deemed 'right' in accordance with custom and origin.

Similarly, human rights understood in this way clearly encourage a one-sided opening up of women's personal rights to freedom. This takes place without concern for the fact that husband and wife together form a single unit, namely a family, the task and harmony of which should stand above the individual rights of man and woman, made autonomous members of society. The prevalent view in Europe is that religion is merely a personal matter. In accordance with this the individual is virtually compelled to lapse from his faith or to change his religion or confession without any restrictions. Here he can even appeal to the basic laws, without taking the social consequences sufficiently into consideration. Beyond doubt the foundation of these rights at an international and human level can be recognized. However, it must also be said openly that most recently above all the view of the 'West' has strongly moulded and controlled the principles of human rights and their vocabulary. By contrast, the socialist states (e.g. the former USSR) had reservations about accepting the European view of numerous human rights – for example political freedom and how it is dealt with.

Exclusively European concepts were used for the composition and vocabulary of the Declaration on Human Rights. Although an international charter should display an international character and embrace the whole of humankind, in fact here many cultures and other communities of peoples had no influence on the formulation of the principles, the vocabulary or the definition of the content of the terms. A worldwide involvement would certainly have been a better guarantee that the charter had a truly international character, and would also have helped towards its acceptance by all of humankind.

So although we Muslims pay our full respects to the international charter of human rights and although we grant that most legal terms in the two UNO agreements of 1966 (on political and civil and on social and economic rights) correspond with the Islamic conception, it still seems necessary to us that we should make clear the basis on which Islam judges human rights and all the basic rights of human beings. After we have already looked at the foundations of human rights in Islam, I would like primarily to consider with the Cairo Declaration on Human Rights in Islam. This declaration, which was promulgated in Cairo on 5 August 1990, can be regarded as a serious attempt to bring together the concepts of Islam in this connection in a convention to be observed by the states and governments of the 'Islamic Conference'. However, the Cairo Declaration is not the only one that we must cite when we speak of basic rights as Islam defines them.

II. The principles of the Islamic idea of human rights

After the revelation of the Holy Book at the beginning of the seventh century to the last of God's messengers, the prophet Muhammad, had been conveyed and completed, a great revolution in knowledge took place within the rapidly growing Islamic community. In fact the Qur'an discloses the foundation of all knowledge that is essential for human life. As a book it not only contains Islamic doctrine along with other values but rather comprises all the knowledge that is fundamental and significant for human progress. In addition to monotheism and the postulate of the exclusive worship of God it creates a complete moral system for human beings and sets down the foundations of the world order for humankind. There are dogmas, ethics, history, wisdom sayings and legislation in the Qur'an. It is on this foundation that the Muslims constructed many sciences which in fact have their origin in the Qur'an. The Qur'an is the work which has uniquely and incomparably shaped the Islamic spirit. Its concepts and images dominate Islamic thought. The Islamic thought material of the verses of the Qur'an and the authentic tradition of the prophet which clarify the verses and lead to action based on them are the two sources which explain the special features of the Islamic understanding of human rights.

1. Man as God's representative on earth

According to the Holy Book, man is God's representative on earth. He was honoured with the task of proclaiming all over the world that worship is due to God alone and that justice, wellbeing and peace are to be established on earth ['When your Lord said to the angels: "I am placing on the earth one who shall rule as My deputy," they replied: "Will You put there one that will do evil and shed blood, when we have for so long sung Your praises and sanctified your name?" He said, "I know what you know not."' (The Cow, v. 30)]. God gave Adam all the concepts, in other words, God endowed him with reason, the capacity for discernment and the drive to gain knowledge.

So on the basis of an explicit statement in the Qur'an, man is God's representative on earth. Moreover he is the only creature which God shapes with his own hand, by breathing into him something of his own spirit. Man is the only creature which God has enabled on the basis of reason to fulfil his exalted task with the necessary physical, mental and spiritual qualities.

In Islam, man is completely in the service of God. Outside this 'devotion' to God all men are born equal and have the same worth, without respect to race and skin colour, social and economic status ['Men, we have created you from a male and a female, and made you into nations and tribes, that you might get to know one another (on the basis of genealogical relationships)' (The Chambers, v. 13)]. This particular verse of the Qur'an is regarded as the basis of the equality of all human beings and is evidence that separation by colour of skin and race is ruled out.

Rule belongs to God alone, for the principles for moral life in society are of his ordaining. Man is obligated to act in accordance with these principles so that he can realize his happiness in this world and in the beyond. Rule here does not mean the direct exercising of power. Rather, it works through the ordering of principles and precepts which are necessary for the legitimate life of human beings in society. No society can survive without a form of rule which regulates human affairs in accordance with the guidance of divine law. The ruler must refer to the divine law and act in accordance with the will of men and their decision. Already in the early period of Islam it was clear to the Muslims that the one in power is a ruler who is commissioned by the community and who works for it. He is someone in their service who accedes to its will. He manages its affairs and exercises his power in consultation with the citizens, listening to their desires and concerns. He does not represent 'divine power' on earth but simply human beings.

Human freedom in Islam is a means towards material and spiritual process. However, it is not to be a freedom without responsibility, merely with an eye to fleshly enjoyment. Rather, Islamic freedom amounts to a capacity for achievement which enables a person to do what is useful for both the individual and for society.

In Islam, the woman is the other half of the man; both are created from one being ['Men, have fear of your Lord, who created you from a single soul (i.e. from the first man, namely Adam). From that soul He created its mate, and through them he bestrewed the earth with countless men and women. Fear God, in whose name you plead with one another, and honour the mothers who bore you (i.e. make sure that you do does not offend against the ties of blood relationship)' (Women, v. 1).] Husband and wife form a unit as a family, which in turn brings together the interests of both partners if each fulfils his or her duty and takes responsibility for their life together.

2. Responsibility for the community

In Islamic society people live together like brothers; they cultivate relations with one another and help one another out of concern for the good and the fear of God. This brotherliness ensures that mutual obligation and mercy become a human right. Therefore individual members of society guarantee that they will help each other in case of distress or need. This common responsibility is counted as one of the pillars of Islam and one of its unshakeable social concepts. It is a responsibility which covers all the needs of life, namely money, knowledge and good advice. It is available to anyone, child or adult, man or woman. This mutual guarantee is not limited to the Muslim but is anyone's human right generally, regardless of race or faith. The Caliph 'Omar Ibn Al-Haṭṭāb also pledged himself for the life of needy non-Muslims. Not to take care of people or people in need was an injustice that was not to be tolerated.

So society is a living being. It is influenced by the behaviour of each individual. Every society has the right to enjoy itself in peace and security and to reject the causes of unrest and corruption. At every point of time and everywhere Islam has been extremely concerned to satisfy the needs of all human beings, i.e. their life, reason, honour and possessions. So in the revealed law of Islam there is a firm connection between the ap-propriateness of accusation and punishment on the one hand and the preservation of the basic interests of the individual on the other. In accordance with the principle of prevention rather than punishment, Islam therefore lays down strict penalties only for a few crimes. These penalties simply serve the purpose (the good purpose) of being a deterrent against murder, theft and adultery. However, the Qur'an requires that extreme precautions should be taken particularly over the inflicting of such punishments and lays down carefully thought out regulations about the nature of the proof which is acceptable in the case of such crimes. The crimes to which strict penalties apply are all acts which without legal sanctions would violate human life, human dignity and property. By contrast, Islamic law leaves it to the secular legislature to punish other criminal offences which do damage to the individual, the state and society. It is for the legislature to impose appropriate punishments depending on the time, the place and the society. Furthermore, Islamic law provides for a deterrent punishment only in the case of those crimes which violate the personal right to life and property and with a view to the preservation of the principle of reason and honour. Moreover in practice such punishments – which are corporal punishments – carry with them guarantees to the advantage of the perpetrator or the accused. Only when the case has been fully examined and there can be no excuse, and the perpetrator has really deserved the punishment, is the punishment in fact inflicted – in the interest of the citizen and to protect the society.

3. God as the guarantor of human rights

I have already indicated the basic concepts of Islam which regard human beings as God's successors on earth and husband and wife as the main cell of life in society. Both partners in marriage are given duties and rights which can make it possible for them to fulfil their task in this world ['Women shall with justice have rights (in the way in which they are treated by men) similar to those exercised against them' (The Cow, v. 228)]. On the other hand, the attitude of Islam to those in power and their right to hold power is that they are the representatives of the community and its servants. Their concern is to order the affairs of the community in accordance with the divine distribution of justice and with the support of others, to whom they are to listen and whom they are to ask for advice. The attitude of Islam to the concept of human freedom, namely that freedom is the most precious thing that a person possesses, challenges the conception that evildoers and blasphemers have advanced. Their misguided understanding of freedom keeps people from progress and makes them incapable of handing down the message of succession on earth and achieving its fulfilment.

III. All the human rights in Islam

From such principles it is possible to derive a number of rights which God has granted to all his servants, as he has shown his appreciation of them only by virtue of their humanity ['We have bestowed blessings on Adam's children' (The Night Journey, v. 70)].

1. *God as giver of human rights*

According to Islamic legislation all human rights come from God. They are neither a gift from man to man, nor are they in the possession of some creature who sometimes gives them and sometimes withholds them (wrongly). The provisions of Islamic legislation with respect to human rights and their extent and its readiness to observe them does not in fact lag behind the progressive international conventions. In the Qur'an human rights are revealed as clear and decisive verses. They are supported by religious and moral guarantees, quite apart from the legal punishment to be imposed on those supposed to have transgressed or misused them. There is no doubt that a critical discussion of Islamic human rights on the basis of Islamic legislation and the principles already mentioned will prove to be a religious, moral and legal necessity within the human community. On closer investigation it is clear that in the case of at least some human rights, their true concept is defined more precisely in the Qur'an.

Both the Qur'an and the Sunna (the tradition of the sayings and actions of the Prophet) indicate a series of rights which God gave as rights for human beings in society. All the human rights produced by the international conventions and agreements are in reality also part of the collection of basic Islamic human rights. It can even be asserted that the concept of 'human rights' in most recent times expresses traditional rights which Islam once professed. In the time of the prophet and under the leadership of his first successors these rights became pre-eminently and completely valid. It will certainly not be difficult for present Islamic society to restore them, following the model of that time.

2. *The concrete rights*

However, the possibility cannot be ruled out of adding these rights to fundamental human rights, with the conception of which in principle they indeed correspond. For the right to the inviolability of privacy, family, home and correspondence (§12 of the Universal Declaration of Human Rights) goes with the 'principle of freedom'. The same is true of freedom of movement and residence (§13 of the Declaration). Furthermore, the right to take part in the government of one's country (§21) belongs with the 'principle of advice and co-operation'. The right to a respectable standard of living adequate for the health and wellbeing of the family (§25) can be put under the 'principle of social solidarity in Islam', as can the right to education (§26). Moreover, one might mention with pride that the content of §1 of the 1948 Declaration, namely the right to have one's human dignity respected, is simply a human repetition of what was proclaimed by the Qur'an more than 1400 years ago ['We have bestowed blessings on Adam's children' (The Night Journey, v. 70)].

It makes sense to point out that with respect to the Islamic fundamental rights mentioned above and concepts of human rights, it is quite possible to frame an Islamic charter of human rights which has a comprehensive humane character worldwide. Islam endorses the basic presupposition of the unity of humankind. ['Men, have fear of your Lord, who created you from a single soul (i.e. from the first man, namely Adam). From that soul He created its mate, and through them he bestrewed the earth with countless men and women. Fear God, in whose name you plead with one another, and honour the mothers who bore you (i.e. make sure that you do not offend against the ties of blood relationship)' (Surah, Women, v. 1).]

This confirms, without any ambiguity, that human beings have human dignity simply by virtue of their being human. The verses of the Qur 'an on basic human rights are to be understood as principles for the human community. For life in community rests on human respect, the guarantee of freedom, the equality of human beings and the safeguarding of social justice, and finally on an exchange of views and joint discussion about the affairs of society. In addition to this, Islamic law guarantees the rights of the individual citizen and the inviolability of private life, property and the dignity of women. There is no limit on the acquisition of property, and freedom of movement and participation in the development of society are permissible. It can only be to the benefit of society if citizens use their energy and intellectual potential on its behalf. The Islamic Conference already published a document on human rights in Islam at its conference in Cairo on 5 August 1990.

IV. The basic right to life and respect

In the Islamic view, man is the most noble and honourable of beings. He has control over everything in heaven and earth and has been given the capacities of reason, thought and guidance through God's grace. In Islam human dignity is based on a closed system. And this very point distinguishes it from the limited Western conception.

1. *Everything at the service of human rights*

Respect for man can be explained and justified in all its aspects from the fact that everything in heaven and earth is at his disposal ['He has subjected to you what the heavens and the earth contain' (Kneeling, v. 13)].

On the other hand, man is the creation of God. He, God, created man with his own hand, gave him a breath of his soul and made him in the most beautiful form ['We created man in a most noble image' (The Fig, v. 4)]. Respect for other human beings is of such significance that the life of an individual is almost equivalent to the life of the human race generally and its ongoing existence ['Whoever kills a human being (and) not say (for vengeance) for someone (others who have been killed by him) or (as a punishment for) disaster (that he has wrought) on earth shall be looked upon as though he had killed all mankind; and whoever saved a human life shall be regarded as though he had saved all mankind' (The Table, v. 32)].

All actions which humiliate or scorn human beings, torture, attacks on the person, mutilation even after death – respect for the human body extends beyond death even in war and in battle conditions, are forbidden. Once the Prophet stopped as the funeral cortege of a Jew went past. His companions were amazed at this and asked why he did it. It is well known that the Jews cherished hatred against Islam and its followers. The Prophet said, 'Is it not perhaps a soul?' That is a clear explanation of the divine respect for human beings as it is revealed in the Qur'an.

2. *Preservation of human dignity*

In keeping with its concern for the preservation of human life, Islam legitimates war only when it is waged in defence of a right and when it has been preceded by a warning and a public declaration. Islam prohibits engaging in war for the sake of plunder, out of nationalistic fanaticism, racial hatred or religious zeal. Limits are put to warlike action. There are examples of this in the tradition. There are prohibitions against the killing of non-combatants, i.e. women, children, and clergy who are devoting themselves to their religious duties. Even those workers who are working away from the theatre of war, for example farmers, are exempt from the killing as long as they are not engaged in the conflict. It is also forbidden to destroy the harvest or cattle. The aim of this precaution was to maintain the food supply. Two outstanding examples have been handed down in connection with conduct in war and the morality of battle by the Prophet himself. Once, when he opposed the killing of a woman and protested to his companions: 'She truly did not fight.' And another time, when he gave the people of Mecca the food that they needed although they had been hostile to him and at war with him. Harsh penalties were imposed as a deterrent on attacks on human life (which were frequent) ['We decreed to them a life for a life, an eye for an eye, a nose for a nose, an ear for an ear, a tooth for a tooth and a wound for a wound' (The Table b.45)]. Conditions and guarantees for this are to be found in the religious law of Islam for each individual case.

In order to preserve the human person and not shame the human body, Islam prohibits suicide ['Do not destroy yourselves, God is merciful to you' (Women, v. 29)]. Similarly, Islam prohibits people from casting themselves into destruction ['And do not with your own hand cast yourselves into destruction' (The Cow, v. 195)].

Because of the dignity of human reason and because this reason is in a position to comprehend the Islamic law, Islam forbids wine; for this drink affects the understanding and damages perception and the capacity for discernment. It similarly forbids anything that damages human reason or weakens human intellectual capacities. Islamic legal scholars have recognized the significance of reason and the capacity for discernment, and their influence on human life. Both gifts are often compared with the religious law; they guide people along the right way. Gazzali, one of the greatest Islamic scholars, says, 'Reason is the law from within, and the religious law is reason from without.' Law and understanding together are the lamps which light men's way in life.

In its respect for human beings and with reference to the integrity of body and senses Islam also prescribes that human beings should avoid certain things that could harm them. It proves to be extremely strict over torture, degradation and humiliation, whether through hurtful words or mockery ['Believers, let no man mock another man, who may perhaps be better than himself. Let no woman mock another woman, who may perhaps be better than herself' (The Chambers, v. 11)]. The same goes for the corpse. One may not degrade or treat with contempt the body of another person. One should wash a corpse, put it in a shroud and carry it to the grave after a special prayer. So the regulations of Islamic law guarantee the whole of a man's being and protect it: what is meant is his soul, his body, his spiritual power and his sensibilities. This article would not be adequate if it did not say something about the manifold aspects of protection and respect for human life.

Man is God's representative on earth. God spoke to the angels and said, 'I appoint a representative on earth'. The representative appointed by God on earth is an honour for human beings and at the same time a task and a distinction, so that men worship God and honour him and fill the earth with the true and the good and with peace. All this can be focussed further on a concern for freedom, equality and brotherhood (solidarity) as these are guaranteed in Islam. For reasons of space it has been necessary here to keep to the basic principles of the Islamic understanding of human rights.

Translated from the Arabic by Habib Jaoiche and from the agreed German text by John Bowden (quotations from the Qur'an are from the English translation by N. J. Dawood, Harmondsworth 1956 with the author's glosses in brackets). For editorial reasons it was necessary to make considerable cuts in the text.

The 1981 'Universal Islamic Declaration of Human Rights': A Christian Reaction

Heiner Bielefeldt

I. Human rights – the universal ethic of modern freedom

As the very term indicates, human rights make a claim to universal validity: they are to apply to all people in the world, regardless of the colour of their skin, their gender and their religious conviction. Human rights follow from the insight that all human beings are 'equal in dignity and rights', as the 1948 United Nations Declaration on Human Rights puts it. More specifically, human rights aim at the recognition and implementation of equal rights to freedom for all men and women. This universal right to freedom is historically new. Though their prehistory may go far back in tradition, human rights first emerge as political demands in the eighteenth century. And only after the Second World War did they find entry into international law.

By contrast, the ethics of the great world religions, including Christianity and Islam, are vastly older. This simple fact already shows that one cannot simply 'derive' human rights from the ethical traditions of the religions. These may have prepared the way for human rights in central aspects, for example in proclaiming the unassailable dignity of human beings. However, there is no disputing the fact that human rights often had to be fought for even against the religious communities. For these communities often contributed towards preserving one-sided relationships of power in state and society. Only in the twentieth century did the Christian churches in principle open up to the claim to freedom expressed in human rights, which previously they had rejected or even condemned. For the Catholic church this happened in John XXIII's encyclical *Pacem in terris* and in the declaration of the Second Vatican Council on religious freedom.

Given the churches' long 'history of suffering' over human rights, Christians have every reason to be cautious in judging other religions and their position on human rights. However, caution and criticism are not mutually exclusive. For the opposite to cultural imperialism is not uncritical indifference to others, but committed dialogue. This is particularly the case in connection with human rights, which, in a world which is increasingly becoming more multicultural and multireligious, are perhaps the only chance of guaranteeing a life for individuals and societies which is worth living. They represent a challenge to all peoples, cultures and religious communities and require of them a readiness for dialogue, criticism and self-criticism. This is the spirit in which I want to go on to make some comments on the 1981 'Universal Islamic Declaration of Human Rights'.

II. An evaluation of the 1981 'Universal Islamic Declaration of Human Rights'

1. Difficulties in assessing the text

It is not easy to form a judgment on the declaration. The difficulties begin with the fact that there are different versions of the text, namely an Arabic original and versions in English and French.[1] All the versions should be equally authentic, but they differ considerably. Roughly speaking, the differences are that the Arabic text brings out the genuinely Islamic character of the text more strongly than the English or French variants. For example, the Arabic text regularly legitimates the human rights cited with quotations from the Qur'an and sayings of the Prophet Muhammad; these quotations are absent from the English and French versions. In what follows I shall keep to the longer Arabic text.[2]

The binding character of the document is also questionable. The title 'Universal Islamic Declaration of Human Rights' could give the impression that the text had been composed in the name of all Islam and applied to all Muslims. However, over against this it has to be stressed that Sunni Islam does not recognize an official teaching office which could make doctrinal decisions binding on the Islamic community. The 'Islamic Council for Europe' which promulgated the declaration is merely a private umbrella organization of European Muslims. It does not even represent all the Muslims living in Europe, far less Islam throughout the world. Moreover there are some Muslims, above all liberal Muslim thinkers, who

have made critical comments on the Islamic Declaration of Human Rights
or have personally distanced themselves from it.[3] The Declaration is not
binding in the legal sense – any more than is the 'Declaration of Human
Rights in Islam' which was promulgated in August 1990 by the Organization of the Islamic Conference in Cairo. This does not exclude the
possibility that such declarations may indirectly have some legal effect by
influencing the legislation or jurisdiction of Islamic states.

2. The problem of the Shariʿa

We now move to the structure and content of the Declaration. At first
glance it is like other catalogues of human rights: it contains an
introduction, an extended preamble and a list of individual rights in
twenty-three articles divided into sub-sections. These include not only
liberal and political but also economic and social rights: the rights to life,
freedom, equality, justice, a fair trial, protection from torture; the right to
asylum, a role in political decisions, freedom of belief, freedom of opinion,
protection of property, the right to work, rights for the family, and so on.

But on closer inspection the text is very different from the United
Nations documents on human rights because of its marked religious
stamp. The very first sentence in the preamble refers to the Qur'an as the
source of the Islamic understanding of human rights: 'Fourteen centuries
ago Islam comprehensively and fundamentally laid down "human rights"
as a law.' The individual articles not only contain numerous quotations
from the Qur'an and sayings of the Prophet but also keep referring to the
Shariʿa, the Islamic legal tradition. Moreover, in many places the term
'umma' is used, which traditionally denotes both the religious and the
political community. Thus for example the right to involvement in politics
is related to the umma (cf. Article 11). Finally, in the section on economic
rights there is also mention of the Islamic 'alms tax' (zakat, cf. Article 15).

How are we to assess the combination of human rights and elements of
Islamic law? Are human rights in this way being commandeered by Islam?
Does the claim that they are universal, and therefore should apply to all
human beings throughout the world, get lost in an exclusively Islamic
framework of reference? Or could the acceptance of the declaration of
human rights conversely lead to new interpretations of the Islamic law?
These questions cannot be answered easily. The concept and the content
of the Shariʿa are anything but clear. Contrary to a widespread understanding in the West, the Shariʿ is in no way a fixed and rigid law, which can be
applied uniformly all over the Islamic world. On the contrary, most legal
schools have always practised a very flexible and pragmatic interpretation
which meets the needs and weaknesses of men and women and also takes

into account particular social circumstances.[4] In Islam there is a living tradition of tolerance, generosity and humanitarian pragmatism. It is based not least on the Qur'an saying that God wants to make it easy for people to fulfil his commands. The divine command is not meant to be a burden but a help.

Nevertheless, it cannot be disputed that the Shari'a in its traditional form contravenes the United Nations norms for human rights at central points. Nor is this surprising. For the Shari'a, of which the Qur'an and the Sunna are the most important sources, is in the end around a thousand years older than human rights. Measured by the recognized standard of international human rights, three points above all are problematical: (a) the cruel corporal punishments which the Shari'a provides for some crimes; (b) the unequal status of husband and wife; and (c) limitations on freedom of religion.[5] Let us now go critically through the Universal Islamic Declaration of Human Rights, paying particular attention to these areas of conflict.

3. Points of conflict

(a) Corporal punishment

In the West, people primarily associate with the term Shari'a a rigid penal law which is characterized by cruel corporal punishments like amputation, flogging and stoning. However, this picture of the Shari'a is very one-sided, and is really a caricature. Certainly corporal punishment is an element of the traditional Shari'a. But by very high requirements for proof which are almost impossible to meet and other means, already in the past attempts were made to see that in many places such punishment was virtually never applied. Rather, it was regarded more as a religious-ethical 'admonition' than as a practicable penal law. Nowadays as a rule no provision for such punishment is made in the penal law-codes of the Islamic states. However, in recent years amputation and other forms of corporal punishment have been reintroduced as a penalty. This is also practised in some Gulf states.

Given this situation, a clear prohibition against such cruel forms of punishment by the Islamic Universal Declaration of Human Rights would surely have been helpful. However, those who framed it regrettably shrank from doing this, probably because some of the corporal punishments (not stoning) are in fact mentioned in the Qur'an. However, the Declaration does contain the recommendation of the Prophet Muhammad that these harsh punishments should not be applied if at all possible (cf. Article 5, clause d). Here it takes up the traditional humane pragmatism of the Shariʿa, without resolutely developing it further in the direction of modern notions of law.

(b) Discrimination against women

Discrimination against women is a main problem in human rights all over the world – even in the societies of the West with their Christian stamp. Like Christianity, Islam grants man and woman equal dignity; however, this does not lead in any way to equal rights. Although historically speaking the Shariʿa clearly improved the legal position of the woman, the woman is discriminated against above all in family law, which lies at the heart of the norms of the Shariʿa that still apply today. In the marriage contract as a rule she is still represented by her male relatives, and in the family is subject to the rule of her husband. In a divorce she is at a disadvantage and inherits less than a male heir of the same degree of affinity would receive. One could also cite further examples.

This traditional superiority of the man to the woman is not fundamentally questioned in the Universal Islamic Declaration of Human Rights. Perhaps it is even further reinforced, in that Article 19, clause a, states that the father makes the decisions about bringing up the children. Here too we have evidence of the conservative spirit of the Declaration, which seeks to avoid any break with tradition. By contrast, there is slight progress in the prohibition of any marriage against the will of bride or bridegroom (cf. Article 19, clause i). Furthermore, it is remarkable that the Declaration always speaks of the woman in the singular in the sections on marriage and family. This gives the impression that monogamous marriage is now presupposed as the normal family model. In fact polygamy, which is still theoretically possible in most Islamic countries, has become unusual in many places.

(c) Complete freedom for religion?

As for relations with other religions, Christians need to recognize self-critically that traditionally Islam has practised a higher degree of tolerance than Christianity. There are even historical examples of Christian minorities who readily submitted to Muslim rule in order to escape extermination by their fellow-Christians!

However, according to traditional interpretation this proverbial Islamic tolerance was limited to adherents of the 'religions of the book', i.e. above all Jews and Christians, and they too had to suffer certain social and legal discrimination, some aspects of which still apply today. Thus in most

Islamic countries it is still legally impossible for a non-Muslim to marry a Muslim wife. A further limit to tolerance was apostasy from Islam, which traditionally was regarded as a crime worthy of death. Even now, in many Islamic countries people who convert from Islam to another religion have to expect grave social and legal consequences, for example the forcible dissolution of their marriages and a loss of parental custody. Executions of 'apostates' are known recently from Iran and the Sudan.

The text of the Universal Islamic Declaration of Human Rights also remains very vague over freedom of religion. For all the respect that is shown to the statements of other religions, it evidently does not go beyond the bounds of the traditional conception of tolerance. Granted, it refers to the Qur'anic saying that there is no compulsion in religion (cf. Article 10, clause a). But at the same time it qualifies religious freedom of confession by saying that this must remain within the framework of the Shari'a and may not weaken the community (*umma*, cf. Article 12, clause a). There is no consideration of current burning problems like mixed marriages and conversion.

III. Perspectives for the future

The Universal Islamic Declaration of Human Rights thus proves on the whole to be a conservative document not free from apologetic and integralistic features. It gives no impetus towards bold reinterpretations and reforms. But at the same time it is evidence that the concept of human rights has meanwhile been accepted in circles of conservative Islamic orthodoxy. As the Shari'a has long been usually interpreted and applied in a flexible way, there is still hope that in time it can be further extended and opened up as a result of thought in terms of human rights. At any rate, one finds a few signs of hope for this in the Declaration. Thus the preamble contains a clear condemnation of slavery – although the traditional Shari'a had a wealth of legal rulings on slavery. Perhaps over and above this we can read out of the Declaration an implicit plea for the suspension of corporal punishment and possibly also a cautious encouragement of reforms in family law.

However, Muslim reformers – like Muhammad Talbi, Muhammad Charfi, Abdulahi Ahmed An-Na'im and many others say that they are not content with such small steps. They call for a resolute reinterpretation of the Shari'a, extending beyond the limits of the classical exposition of the law. Here they are not just seeking to make space for reforms over human rights. Rather, at the same time they see the law as an opportunity to open up the original sense of the Shari'a again, perhaps in a deeper way. For

Shariʿa literally does not mean law but 'guidance'. Thus, as Muhamad Said al-Ashmawy stresses, to liberate the Shariʿa from superficial politicizing and from being overloaded with a mediaeval legalism is a genuine religious task.[6] For, he argues, this is the presupposition for a regaining of the original ethical and spiritual dimension of the Shariʿa.

Thus a bold openness towards the modern world and human rights could prove to be an opportunity for faith. That is true not only for Islam but similarly for Christianity.

Translated by John Bowden

Notes

1. Cf. Ann Elizabeth Mayer, *Islam and Human Rights. Tradition and Politics*, San Francisco and London 1991, 27.

2. Here I am following the translation (with introduction and commentary) by Martin Frostner, CIBEDO-Dokumentation no. 15/16, Frankfurt am Main 1982.

3. Cf. the article by Ali Merad in Johannes Schwartländer (ed.), *Freiheit der Religion. Christentum und Islam unter der Herausforderung der Menschenrechte*, Mainz 1993.

4. Cf. Joseph Schact, *An Introduction to Islamic Law*, Oxford 1964.

5. Cf. Sami A. Aldeeb Sahlieh, 'La définition internationale des droits de l'homme et l'islam', *Revue générale de droit international public*, 1968, 625–716.

6. Cf. Muhammad Said al-Ashmawy, *L'islamisme contre l'islam*, Paris 1992.

Is Islamic Revelation an Abrogation of Judaeo-Christian Revelation? Islamic Self-identification in the Classical and Modern Age

Abdulaziz Sachedina

I. Religious exclusivisms

Religious systems have traditionally claimed absolute devotion and exclusive salvation history for themselves. Such insistence on salvific authenticity and exclusivist claim were regarded as natural and necessary instruments for self-identification of a group against other claims of absolute truth. Moreover, this claim was found to be effective in providing legitimating and integrative discourse that furnished its members with practical means of asserting their collective communal identity. In addition, the newly fostered communal identity provided an equally effective basis for aggression and exploitation of those who did not share this sense of solidarity with the community of the believers. Rationalization of the aggression, characterized in religious terms as a 'holy war', made it possible for the believers of a given system to impose their hegemony over the 'infidels' in the name of some sacred authority by use of force.

To be sure, religious legitimation of such hegemonic interests and methods were questionable and hence had to be justified by means of and sought in the scriptures which appeared to deny any claim to its compulsive devotion and its defence of the prohibitive social and legal structures built upon religious absolutism. It was this intellectual process of legitimation that produced the exegetical devices to extrapolate or even interpolate the revelational sources to provide a convincing

statement of exclusive religious claim to absolute truth. More pertin-
ently, exegesis of specific passages of the scripture provided the restrictive definition of soteriological faith in which other religions were
systematically excluded as being superseded and, consequently, their
ability to lead a believer to salvation was seen as being ineffective.

II. The uniqueness of divine revelation

The religious experience of Muslims in history clearly shows the
endeavours of some classical Muslim exegetes of the Qur'an to separate
the salvation history of the community from other Abrahamic faiths by
attesting to the superseding validity of the Islamic revelation over
Christianity and Judaism. In an attempt to demand unquestioning
acceptance of the new faith, Muslim exegetes had to devise termino-
logical as well as methodological stratagems to circumscribe those verses
of the Qur'an which tended to underscore its ecumenical thrust by
extending salvific authenticity and adequacy to other monotheistic traditions.

Thus, for instance, Islam introduced a universal discourse relating all
humanity to the unique and single divine authority, thereby relativizing
all the competing claims to the human search for exclusive reality. This
universal idiom was based on the principle of *tawḥīd* — the affirmation
of divine unity. The acknowledgment of *tawḥīd* signified a transformation of human focus on self to the Self, the ultimate Reality, the Source
of all other selves. It affirmed the centrality of God without human
mediation in negotiating human-God relationship and the spiritual
destiny of humankind. *Tawḥīd*, moreover, uniquely placed God as the
source of revelation communicated through the *prophets*. The prophets
represented basically one and the same revelation that embodied the
divine will at different times.

However, as Islam laid the foundation of its political order, Muslim
leaders sought out particular integrative discourse that furnished the
believers with a unique identity and a practical means of asserting it
through the creation of exclusive order based on declaration of faith, the
shahāda. This development marked a clear shift from the Qur'anic
recognition of religious pluralism in the sense of God-centred particular
human religiosity (within each instance of historical revelation of the
divine reality) and the unity of humankind at the level of universal
moral-spiritual discourse. Political Islam was an important phase in
Muslim self-identification as a community endowed with specific salvific
efficacy in its tradition. Moreover, in the sectarian milieu of seventh-

century Arabia early Muslims encountered competing claims to authentic religion by other monotheists like the Christians and the Jews. This encounter, which produced inter-religious polemic, in addition to the establishment of Islamic public order where Muslims enjoyed a privileged position, led to the notion of independent status of Islam as a unique and perfect version of the original Abrahamic monotheism. The universally accepted notion that emerged from these polemics was the doctrine that the Qur'anic revelation completed the previous revelations, which had no more than a transitory condition and a limited application. Such a notion also led to the doctrine of supersession among some Muslim theologians, who argued that neither the Mosaic law intended for exclusively Jewish use, not the Christian scripture directed towards the children of Israel, had any claim to eternal validity.

The apparent contradiction between some passages of the Qur'an recognizing other authentic salvific sources and others declaring Islam as the sole source of salvation had to be resolved for providing a viable system of peaceful co-existence with these religions. The Qur'anic pluralism is expressed by promising salvation to, at least, 'whoso believes in God and the Last Day' among 'those of Jewry, and the Christians, and those Sabaeans'. (2.62). By contrast, Islamic absolutism is asserted in no uncertain terms, namely that 'whoso desires another religion than Islam, it shall not be accepted of him; in the next world he shall be among the losers.' (3.85). Hence the resolution of the absolutist claim on the one hand and the recognition of the pluralist principle in salvation on the other had enormous implications for the community's relations with other religions in general, and the People of the Book in particular.

III. Are the other religions superseded?

There is no doubt that the Qur'an is silent on the question of the supersession of the previous Abrahamic revelations through the emergence of Muhammad. There is no statement in the Qur'an, direct or indirect, to suggest that the Qur'an saw itself as the abrogator of the previous scriptures. In fact, even when repudiating the distortions introduced in the divine message by the followers of Moses and Jesus, the Qur'an confirms the validity of these revelations and their central theme, namely, 'submission' founded upon sincere profession of belief in God. However, in the classical exegetical literature the question of the chronology of the divine revelation and its applicability for the subsequent communities formed an important theological consideration.

The principle of chronology provided the theologians with the notion of *naskh* (abrogation or supersession) to expound various stages of revelation throughout history. Essentially the same revelation was delivered piecemeal, the later revelation completing and thereby abrogating the previous ones. It is important to bear in mind that the Qur'an introduces the idea of abrogation in connection with legal injunctions revealed in particular verses in which one aspect of legal requirement may be said to be abrogated or superseded by another verse. Accordingly, invoking abrogation in connection with Islam's attitude toward former Abrahamic traditions was, to say the least, inconsistent. Even those classical exegetes like Muhammad b. Jarīr al-Tabarī (died 923), who had supported the principle of chronology to argue for the exclusive salvific efficacy of Islam and its role as the abrogator of the previous monotheistic traditions, could not fail to notice the incongruity of extending the notion of abrogation to the divine promise of rewarding those who believe in God and the Last Day and work righteousness (2.62). In fact, Tabari regards such abrogation as incompatible with the concept of divine justice.[1]

IV. The differences between Muslim interpretations

Nevertheless, those who accepted the notion of supersession of the pre-Qur'anic revelations depended on a tradition reported in many early commentaries on the verse 3.85, which states that no other religion than Islam would be acceptable to God. The tradition purports to establish that 3.85, which was revealed subsequent to 2.62, actually abrogated God's promise to those who acted righteously outside Islam in 2.62. Another Sunni commentator, Isma'īl b. 'Umar ibn Kathīr (died 1373), has no hesitation in maintaining that based on 3.85, nothing other than Islam was acceptable to God after Muhammad was sent. Although he does not appeal to the concept of abrogation as evidence, his conclusions obviously point to the idea of supersession when he states the salvific state of those who preceded Muhammad's declaration of his mission. Ibn Kathīr maintains that the followers of previous guidance and their submission to a rightly guided life guaranteed their way to salvation only before Islamic revelation emerged.[2]

It is clear that the notion of the abrogation of the previous revelation was not universally maintained even by those exegetes who otherwise required, at least in theory, other monotheists to abide by the new Sharīʿa of Muhammad. It is difficult to gauge the level of Christian influence over Muslim debates about the supersession of the previous revelation. It is not far-fetched to suggest that debates about Islam superseding Christianity and Judaism, despite the explicit absence of any reference to them in the Qur'an, must have entered Muslim circles through the most thoroughgoing Christian debates about Christianity having superseded Judaism, more particularly when Christians claimed to be the legitimate heirs to the same Hebrew Bible that was the source of Jewish law.

The Muslim community, with its independent source of ethical and religious prescriptions, the Arabic Qur'an, in addition to its control over the power structure that defined its relationship with others, was in little need of establishing its theory of self-determination from the previous monotheistic traditions with which it never severed its theological connection through Abrahamic salvation history. The Qur'an relates its experience of 'submission to God's will' (*islām*) to Abraham, the 'unitarian' (*muwaḥḥid*), who 'in truth was not a Jew, neither a Christian; but he was a Muslim and one of pure faith; certainly he was never of the idolaters' (3.67).[3]

This Qur'anic spirit of ecumenism within the Abrahamic traditions always remained the latent potential to be expounded at different times in history as the community negotiated its relationship to the power that dominated its destiny. Depending upon the social and political circumstances of the Muslim community during the colonial and post-colonial era, Muslim exegetes have recaptured the Qur'anic pluralistic thrust in varying degrees. In this regard, theological affiliation of the exegetes has played a significant role.

There were essentially two theological positions on the moral and spiritual guidance that God provides to humanity for it to attain salvation. Those theologians who maintained the divine will as all-encompassing and all-omnipotent considered it necessary for humanity to be exposed to revealed guidance through the prophets for its ultimate prosperity. On the other hand, theologians who maintained freedom of human will endowed with necessary cognition to exercise its volition considered the human intellect to be capable of attaining godly life. It is for the most part the latter group, identified among the Sunnites as the Mu'tazilites, and the majority of the Shi'ites, who conceded the continued salvific efficacy of the other monotheistic faiths on the basis of both the revealed and the rational guidance to which the Christians and the Jews were exposed. They regarded the 'People of the Book' (the Jews and the Christians) as responsible for acting upon their revelation, the substance of which has remained recognizable despite the neglect and alteration it has suffered. The former group, on the contrary, postulating a theory of chronological revelation, said that these religions were a source of divine guidance only before the time of Muḥammad. After the emergence of Islam they had to accept Muḥammad as the Prophet in order to be saved.

V. The acknowledgment of other religions

The majority of the modern exegetes of the Qur'an have maintained the Mu'tazilite theological position on human free will. They believe that human beings are adequately endowed with cognition and volition to pursue their spiritual destiny through the revealed message of God. Thus, Muḥammad Rashīd Riḍā (died 1935), reflecting the Mu'tazilite attitude of his teacher, and a prominent Muslim modernist, Muḥammad 'Abduh (died 1905), maintains that human responsibility to God is proportionate to the level of one's exposure to God's purpose about which one is apprised either through revelation or reason. The purpose of revelation is to clarify and elucidate matters that are known through the human intellect. The basic beliefs like the existence of God and the Last Day are necessarily known through it. Prophets come to confirm what is already inspired to the human intellect. Accordingly, there is an essential unity in the beliefs of 'the people of divine religions (*ahl al-adyān al-ilāhīya*)' who have been exposed to the divine guidance as well as an innate disposition to believe in God and the Last Day and do good works.[4]

Moreover, God's promise applies to all who have this divine religion, regardless of formal religious affiliation, for God's justice does not allow favouring one group while ill-treating another. All peoples who believe in a prophet and in the revelation particular to them, 'their wages await them with their Lord, and no fear shall there be on them, neither shall they sorrow' (2.62). Rashīd Riḍā does not stipulate belief in the prophethood of Muḥammad for the Jews and Christians desiring to be saved, and hence implicitly maintains the salvific validity of both the Jewish and Christian revelation.[5]

Among the Shi'ite commentators, Muḥammad Ḥusayn al-Tabatabā'ī (died 1982), following the well-established Shi'ite opinion from the classical age, rejected the notion of the abrogation of divine promise in 2.62. In fact he does not support the supersession of pre-Qur'anic revelations even when he regards them distorted and corrupted by their followers. Nevertheless, he regards the ordinances of the Qur'an as abrogating the laws extracted from the two earlier scriptures. Evidently he confines abrogation to its juridical meaning where it signifies 'repeal' of an earlier ordinance by a fresh ruling because of its inapplicability in changed circumstances. In connection with those passages that supported the ecumenical thrust of the Qur'an, like the verse 2.62, he rebuffed the opinion held by some Muslims that God promises salvation to particular groups because they bear certain names; on the contrary, any one who holds true belief and acts righteously is entitled to God's reward and protection from punishment, as promised in 6.88: 'God has promised those of them who believe and do good, forgiveness and a great reward.'[6]

VI. The Qur'an: no abrogation of the Judaeo-Christian revelation

To recapitulate, in response to the question raised in the title, 'Is Islamic Revelation an Abrogation of Judaeo-Christian Revelation?, it is accurate to maintain that the Qur'an does not see itself as the abrogator of the Judaeo-Christian revelation. Yet some Muslim exegetes of the classical age, who were engaged at one level in providing an exclusive and independent identity for the Muslim *Umma* and at the other in defending Islam's claim to being the unadulterated version of the previous revelations, developed hermeneutical devices to extrapolate such a theological position. Thus in verse 3.85 they took the word *islām* as the proper name of the historical religion brought by Muḥammad rather than as a generic term indicating the act of 'submission' to the will of God. Similarly, the verses that recommended tolerance towards the People of the Book were considered abrogated by the verses requiring *jihad* against them.

To be sure, some Muslim exegetes sought to restrict the universal discourse of the Qur'an that defined a true believer as responding to the essentially twofold aspect of the Abrahamic religions: belief in God and the Last Day, and the praxis based on revealed guidance. It did not insist upon the acceptance of Muḥammad's prophetic mission. Such a requirement was part of the particular discourse of the Muslim *umma*. It was this particular discourse that led to all other religions being regarded as having been superseded and their salvific efficacy invalidated. Yet, within this emerging theological consensus, there was an explicit refusal to restrict the Qur'anic promise of salvation to other monotheists, who have been equally exposed to authentic revelation.

Modern exegetes like Rashīd Riḍā and Ṭabāṭabā'ī represent the unmistakable Qur'anic spirit of God-centred identity for humanity, in which the external form of religion is relegated to the inward witness of the divine that defies any exclusive and restrictive identification. In fact, religious pluralism is seen by the Qur'an as fulfilling some divine purpose for humanity. What matters ultimately is the belief in God who has 'ingrained in the human soul' universally objective values (9.18) that touch all human beings even when they follow their particular revealed paths. The Qur'an admonishes humankind 'to be forward in good work':

To everyone of you (religious communities) We have appointed a law and a way (of conduct). If God had willed He would have made you all one nation (on the basis of that law and that way), but (He did not do so) that He may try you in what has come to you (in the form of revelation); therefore, be you forward (i.e., compete with one another) in good works. Unto God shall you return all together, and He will tell you (the Truth) about what you have been disputing (5.48).

Bibliography

(In addition to works cited in the footnotes)

Mahmoud Ayoub, *The Qur'an and Its Interpreters*, Albany, NY 1984

Jane D. McAuliffe, *Qur'anic Christians: An Analysis of Classical and Modern Exegesis*, Cambridge 1991

Abdulaziz Sachedina, 'Jews, Christians and Muslims According to the Qur'an', *The Greek Orthodox Theological Review* 31, 1986, 105–20

—— 'Universal and Particular Discourse in the Islamic Tradition: A Muslim Response', *Church and Society* 83, 1992, 34–37

Annemarie Schimmel and Abdoldjavad Falaturi (eds.), *We Believe in One God: The Experience of God in Christianity and Islam*, New York 1979

Muzammil H. Siddiqi, 'Muslim and Byzantine Christian Relations: Letter of Paul of Antioch and Ibn Taymiyah's Response', *The Greek Orthodox Theological Review* 31, 1986, 33–45

Notes

1. Tabarī, *Jāmi 'al-bayān 'an ta'wīl āy al-qur'an*, Cairo 1954, II, 155–6.

2. Ibn Kathīr, *Tafsīr al-qur'ān al-'aẓīm*, Cairo 1937, I, 103.

3. For the theological problems faced by early Christianity in declaring its originality and working out its relation to Judaism see Marcel Simon, *Verus Israel: A Study of the Relations between Christians and Jews in the Roman Empire (AD 135–425)*, New York 1986, esp.ch.3.

4. Rashid Ridā, *Tafsīr al-qur'ān al-ḥakīm al-shahīr bi-tafsīr al-manār*, Beirut nd, I, 339.

5. Ibid., 336.

6. Tabātabā'ī, *al-Mizān fī tafsīr al-Qur'ān*, Beirut 1974, I, 193.

Christianity – Challenged by Islam

Gerhard Böwering

I. A changing world in dialogue and collaboration

1. Very different times

The rise of Islam, spearheaded by Muhammad (died 632), was a call to reform that the church, saturated with success after Constantine the Great (died 337), neglected to perceive. Lacking a thorough study of real Islam, with which it rubbed shoulders along the Mediterranean, the mediaeval church, by default, encouraged Islamic structures of community, tradition, law and theology to grow alongside it into a distinct and separate world religion. There were exceptions to the disregard of Islam on the part of the church. A man of monastic peace, Peter the Venerable (died 1156), tried to convert the Crusades into a non-violent missionary venture and ordered the first Latin translation of the Qur'an. The charismatic Francis of Assisi (died 1226) went to Egypt, where the Crusaders were besieging Damietta, and preached in the Sultan's camp. The theologian Thomas Aquinas (died 1274) revitalized Christianity through his intellectual encounter with Islamic philosophy. From his Alpine retreat John of Segovia (died 1456) advocated an approach to Islam by peace and study rather than the sword. After the fall of Constantinople to the Turks in 1453, the prophetic visionary Nicholas of Cusa (died 1464) wrote a treatise on the Qur'an and advocated one religion amid all the variety of rites. These voices broke the monotony of a mediaeval church that too often perceived its destiny in ecclesiastical triumph and worldly success and approached the Muslims with the wars of the major crusades (1095–1270).

At the beginning of the modern period came the challenge of the reformation, led by Martin Luther (died 1546), which turned the church to its much-needed inner reform, but did not orient it to initiate the exploration of the world religions, including Islam, in this age of geographical discovery. With the celebration of reason during the

European Enlightenment (seventeenth–eighteenth centuries), the West became even more focused on its own knowledge, freedom and happiness. The military protection of the colonial powers reinforced Western superiority over other civilizations and generated the spirit of missionary activity that sought to bring salvation to the heathens. A mind-set was fostered that made the West the standard of culture and induced the church to see no salvation beyond the confines of its own deposit of faith.

It took until the twentieth century for the church to see itself as a pilgrim people on the way to God, together with the majority of humanity following other religions. From this new angle of self-perception the church is challenged to reject exclusivism and espouse a comprehensive and inclusive faith that opens itself to other cultures and religions. As the church tries to shift from soliloquy to face-to-face colloquy and side-by-side collaboration with other religions at the end of its second millennium, it struggles anew with the crux of religion, the divine-human communication on the meaning of our life and death. In the changing world of today, the global religions are no longer confined within geographical borders. A great migration of people is in progress. The technology of modern communication and rapid international travel make other religions present to us and ours present to them in the global village. In this real-life meeting of world religions, Christianity and Islam, on account of their shared principles of universal outlook and missionary thrust, can both express a growing concern for the world as a whole and see their common roots in the Abrahamic faith.

2. What is real dialogue?

When describing their approach to other world religions, Christians have in recent times begun to speak about 'dialogue' in place of the traditional 'mission'. Despite the many efforts expended on dialogue by both Catholics and Protestants, no comprehensive view of its essence and nature has emerged. It is not clear whether its focus is religious or social or a mixture of both. The indiscriminate use of the word 'dialogue' can foster the fallacious assumption that one method and approach equally applies to all world religions, while giving little regard to the great range of their actual and specific differences. Half-way solutions, such as relativism and syncretism, will not cut the knot where world religions intersect and separate. Dialogue also grapples with suspicions that it is another tactic for the erstwhile mission or a method of self-gain over less experienced partners. Some occasions of dialogue meetings have led to polarized discussions; others have succumbed to the niceties of ping-pong diplomacy. These pitfalls are not absent from Muslim-Christian dialogue. For Christians, the need to protect the significance that Jesus of Nazareth has for all human beings frequently overshadows the belief that all religions enshrine a human response to God's revelation. Accordingly, Muslims tend to perceive dialogue as hidden proselytism and a subtle attempt at conversion. They also perceive a gap separating the potential partners in dialogue, for which Muslims are generally less prepared through attitude and study. If any real dialogue is to come about, it cannot occur in unequal confrontation or compromise but in living witness and honourable conduct toward each other in God's service. It will take time for dialogue to be seen as giving birth to something new, as a creative process of being a man or woman serving God within other cultures or religions.

Dialogue with Christianity or other world religions is not a pressing concern for most Muslims. Some leading Muslim scholars, however, accept a measure of cultural pluralism, aware that Islam cannot exist in isolation in the modern world. They feel that the forces of revival are weighed down by the burden of Islam's mediaeval past, and they see that their stand is engaged in a confrontation with a growing fundamentalist majority. They refer to incidents when Muhammad entered into dialogue with Christians, recall junctures of mediaeval history when Islam was revitalized through encounter with Christian culture, and realize that the modern structures of Islam are established in inevitable contact with the West. As the fruit of their interchange with Western scholars, they desire to gain practical know-how, not religious gnosis. By acquiring tools and instruments, such as critical method, source criticism and computer programmes for text analysis, they hope to develop their own perspective on Islamic religious history. Forging their own solutions to the problems of modernity rather than copying ours, they would be empowered to orchestrate a genuine reformation of Islam. To put it in contrasting language: Christians seek religious dialogue, Muslims desire scholarly collaboration.

II. Islam and Christianity

Muslim apologetics and Christian polemics (or vice versa), developed in mediaeval times and repeated until today, focus on the central dogmas of Trinity, incarnation and redemption, but miss the point because neither meets the other on its own ground. The pattern lives on in the widely intransigent attitude toward Islam on the part of the oriental churches in the Middle East, born of great isolation, long suffering and fear for survival in the face of an often intolerant Muslim majority. 'Love the Muslims but not Islam' is an erroneous maxim because it fails to recognize that love must respect the others for what they are at heart and at root. Without love for Islam, Christians will have no access to the truth it holds. The long history of Islam gives testimony to its truth, the religious practice of the Muslims witness to its durability. Islam and Christianity appear as two parallel developments that grow out of a common origin, God's self-revelation to humanity in his Word experienced in monotheistic faith; and speed toward an unknown future and common goal, resurrection. There are stark differences in this parallelism. Christianity experiences itself as mediated by the Word made flesh, Islam puts the believer directly before God as listener of the Word. Christians draw their inspiration from the prayer of Jesus, Abba, 'our Father'; Muslims find their spiritual energy in Allah, the only one who can truly say, Ana, 'I am' (though it is uttered by the human tongue).

1. One in Abraham?

The Abrahamic faith in monotheism unites Judaism, Christianity and Islam as consecutive articulations of trust in God. As Abraham migrated, he broke with the old gods and did not accept the gods of the new land. Rather, he put his trust in the nameless God, beyond all gods and without locale, who had called him out of his land to a new home. This religion of trust in God became the common root of Judaism, the religion of hope; Christianity, the religion of love; and Islam, the religion of faith. Islam sees itself both at the end and beginning of this development. In one sense, Islam is the final link in the chain of the three revealed religions, confirming Torah and Gospel, the messages of Moses and Jesus, through the Qur'an proclaimed by Muhammad. In another sense, Islam goes back behind Judaism and Christianity, undercutting its sibling religions, by tracing its origins to the primaeval religion revealed to Adam and brought back from oblivion by Muhammad, who finds his model in Abraham's submission to the one God.

Since its advent, Islam has been the world religion closest to Christianity in space and time. It has been its geographical neighbour worldwide and its theological twin through the ages. Blinded by their nearness to one another, Muslim and Christian eyes have been unable to perceive precise contours. While Judaism is based on the belief that God has spoken to Israel, his chosen people, Christianity has seen the word of Christ Jesus as the messianic fulfilment of its predecessor, Judaism. Islam, however, has defined itself from the outset as superseding its twin forebears by returning to the original religion of Abraham. Christianity, the middle sibling, views itself as the new covenant with regard to the older sibling, but has been at a loss to define itself towards Islam coming after it. Islam holds the advantageous position of being the last of the three sibling religions that can look at its forebears as history, mere preliminaries to its own full and final universal message. This vision filled Islam with a sense of superiority, steeled by its expansion into an empire that assimilated advanced civilizations that had flourished in territories it came to conquer.

2. Islam and Judaeo-Christianity

The self-perception of Islam as a reform re-establishing the religion of Abraham lends support to a view of the relationship between Islam and early Jewish Christianity that lacks exact historical proof but rests on solid ground of common origin. The church once was a church made up of Jews and Gentiles. Because of historical circumstances (after the destruction of Jerusalem in 70 and the collapse of Bar Kochba's revolt in 135) it evolved in two strands. West of Jerusalem, so to speak, Gentile Christianity turned into Hellenistic Christendom through Paul, the apostle in Greek garb, and developed into the normative church around the core of a Son-of-God theology (including central doctrines such as Trinity, incarnation and redemption). East of the Jordan, Jewish Christianity found a continuation in Semitic Islam through Muhammad, the apostle in Arab dress, and developed the legacy of a Servant-of-God theology (with a focus on an uncompromising monotheism and a vivid eschatology). Without substantial new evidence from archaeological excavations or manuscript discoveries, it will be difficult to draw a line of direct dependence over a hiatus of almost 500 years from Jewish Christianity to Islam. Rather, one will have to acknowledge that heterogeneous traditions reached Muhammad, including not only Jewish Christian (e.g. Elkesaites, Ebionites) but also other marginalized Christian views (e.g. Monarchianism, Sabellianism, Monophysitism, Nestorianism), which had been anathematized by the normative church. The various strands of foreign vocabulary, including Ethiopian terms, in the Qur'an are evidence linking Muhammad with a variety of sectarian traditions.

3. The Qur'anic Jesus

Islam, the youngest of the great world religions and the only one coming after Christianity, adopted a self-conscious attitude towards Christianity from its very origins, not unlike the position Christianity took *vis-à-vis* Judaism, and forged its own image of Jesus, not unlike the way the New Testament cut John the Baptist down to size. The Qur'anic Jesus, called Messiah and God's servant, preached the truth and insisted that he was only a human being. His virgin birth from Mary is a work of divine omnipotence and his power to perform miracles an act of divine permission. Jesus confirmed the divine message sent down to the Jews through Moses and predicted that after him there would come a messenger with a most praiseworthy name. In Muslim understanding this messenger is not the Holy Spirit but Muhammad. The Jews tried to kill Jesus but did not slay or crucify him; they executed another, and God raised his servant to heaven. The mystery surrounding the end of Jesus' life opens the door for his return in parousia, mentioned only cryptically in the Qur'an.

In tradition, *Hadith*, the basic body of religious sources second to the Qur'an, Islam lives in the vivid expectation of Jesus' second coming, ushering in the realm of peace and justice at the end of time, in which Muhammad plays no part. At the end of time, Jesus will descend on the white arcade of the eastern gate at Damascus, in shining clothes, with his head anointed, and a spear in his hand to slay the Antichrist. He will go to Jerusalem, perform the prayer at dawn in Muslim fashion and rid the world of all unbelievers and their symbols. All peoples of the book will believe in him, forming only one community, Islam, and the reign of justice and complete peace will set in. The reign of Jesus, God's glorified servant, will last forty years, followed by the 'Hour', the end of the world on the day when God alone will sit in judgment at the universal resurrection. In Shi'ism, in particular, the utopia at the end of time was linked with the idea of the Mahdi, the restorer of religion and justice, who gloriously rises as the expected ruler issuing from the Prophet's family. This expectation of a restorer of religion, straightening the spine of religion and restoring Islam to its original perfection, became the engine of many renewal movements in Islam.

The Qur'an accepts Christians as 'people of the book', without demanding their conversion to Islam, and cites monks with respect because of their prayer and humility. What the Qur'an most expects from Christians is the witness that there is only one supreme and almighty God – in other words, a genuine recognition of the essential monotheistic message of Islam without any trinitarian misinterpretation. In the Qur'an, Jesus reproaches his own community for the tritheistic notion of God as Father, Mother and Son and explicitly denies his own sonship. The cause of this criticism may not only lie in Muhammad's own misperceptions regarding the Trinity but also in misconceptions of his sectarian informants about God as origin, word and spirit. The same may be said with regard to the interpretation of Jesus's death on the cross, the related notions of incarnation and redemption, or various forms of understanding the Spirit in the Qur'an.

III. Muhammad and the Qur'an

The tension created in these and other questions at variance between the two religions is rooted in the understanding of revelation: the Islamic conception is static, the Christian dynamic. Islam does not share the Christian view of progressive revelation in nature, the history of Israel, the person of Jesus of Nazareth, the events of this age and the signs of the times. Islam makes a categorical distinction between the messenger and the message; for Christianity, the medium is the message. Christianity sees God revealed in the person of Jesus Christ, the word become flesh. For Islam Allah reveals himself in his speech, the word become book, the Qur'an – in other words, *incarnatio* versus *inlibratio*. According to Islam there is only one essential divine revelation, reiterated by the prophets through the ages without any contribution of their own: God is one, Creator of this world and Judge in the world to come. From Adam to Muhammad, the seal of the prophets, the messengers are human beings and divinely chosen mouthpieces of revelation through whom God speaks forth the primordial truth recorded in a heavenly book. God is the sole author of revealed scripture; his word passes untouched through the messenger whom it neither transforms nor divinizes. Since the Qur'an is and remains God's very own words, it includes only God's voice without any human speech added; it literally is God's word, word for word. It holds nothing radically new, because it brings the oldest thing of all, the first proclamation, unknown in the Arabic tongue prior to Muhammad.

On the eve of Islam, polytheism, bound up with tribal groups and local cults, and fatalism, linked with a sense that time erases human works without hope of life beyond death, were no longer adequate to deal with the problems faced by the Arabs. Conversion to Christianity or Judaism, however, meant siding with foreign powers and losing one's autonomy. A needy orphan become Meccan merchant who turned preacher at the age of forty, Muhammad spotted the open middle ground of this Arab dilemma. Christian monks recited their scripture in Aramaic and Jews studied their sacred scrolls in Hebrew; no Arabic translation of the Bible had been made. He would provide the Arabs with a scripture in their own language, the Arabic Qur'an, in style resembling the inspired utterances of the old Arab soothsayers. The decision to proclaim the Qur'an was provoked by Muhammad's profound sense of being called by Allah as his messenger. This prophetical consciousness transformed the forerunners he perceived in sacred history, from Noah and Abraham through Moses and Jesus to heroes of Arab lore, into prototypes of a model: God's deliverance of the messenger. The messenger prevails through the heaven-sent punishment that overtakes his opponents because of their rejection of the message.

Deliverance came to Muhammad at the break point of his life. Accepted by only a small group of followers in Mecca and rejected as a prophet by his tribe, Muhammad began to despair in the slow hand of God's vengeance. In Medina, an oasis at some distance from his home town, warring factions sought out Muhammad as an arbitrator in their disputes with one another and with three small Arabicized Jewish tribes in their midst. Muhammad saw the opportunity and decided to emigrate with his followers to Medina in 622. By this exodus, the *Hegira*, his flock became refugees and dissidents, who had renounced their tribal blood bonds and opened a path for all-out conflict with their Meccan kinsmen. In the ensuing battle at Badr in 624, Muhammad led his followers in an astonishing victory over the Meccans. He was convinced that God had sent deliverance by having his angels join the battle and making him triumph over the unbelievers. The victory was sealed with Muhammad's conquest of Mecca in 630 and the destruction of its idols and images. By the end of his life, Muhammad had become leader of the unified Arabs, their prophet and statesman, in the all-out struggle of jihad. Beginning with the corporate bloodshed at Badr, the history of Islam became bent in the bow of tension between striving for God and struggle for dominion.

The Day of Deliverance had an effect similar to the salvation of Noah's people from the flood and Moses' people from the forces of Pharaoh. It changed the direction of Muhammad's message from a preaching of reform to the founding of a distinct community. Contrary to his expectation, the Jews in Medina had refused to accept the Qur'anic message and its stories of the prophets as a religious confirmation of their Hebrew scriptures. In the light of this rejection, Muhammad changed the *qibla*, the direction of Muslim prayer, from Jerusalem to Mecca, and replaced Ashura with the duty of fasting in Ramadan. The *Kaaba*, the pagan shrine of Mecca, became the ritual centre of the Muslim cult. Standing in the heart of Mecca as House of Allah, it was seen as founded by Abraham, in whom Islam discovered its religious roots and monotheistic origin. The theological reorientation of Islam had serious consequences for its scripture. In a way, the Qur'an itself became the *furqan*, the symbol of separation and deliverance. Before, the Qur'an had been a collection of divine signs of power, memories of old tales and stories of divine punishment, recited in prayer and as an admonition for the present or a reminder of the past. Now, Muhammad came to conceive of it as a book, *kitab*, that would be the source and authority for Islamic religion in belief and practice, similar to the Torah and Gospel in the hands of Jews and Christians. The Holy Book of the Qur'an was born, with its laws and regulations for an ordered community life (though produced in its actual book form after Muhammad's death). The Qur'an as recited word of God lives on in the daily ritual of Islamic prayer, in which the Muslim comes closer to God than anywhere else.

IV. Islamic prayer, time and thought

1. Islamic prayer
Islamic prayer is more than reciting the Qur'an; it constitutes the concrete expression of submission to God in the daily life of Muslim society. While Christians experience liturgical prayer as a mediation of God's love, Muslims see their ritual prayer as an act of obedience to God in content, mode and timing. The Muslim enters into prayer with the help of his ear and heart, by listening to the recited word of the Qur'an and giving witness, through symbolic gestures of surrender, to the divine majesty it enunciates. The ritual prayer of Islam, *salat*, is composed of two principal elements, bodily acts of submission before God, expressed through standing, bowing and prostration, and an actual listening to Qur'an recital in obedience to his word at five precise times of the day. In prayer, the Muslim is hearer of the divine word *par excellence*: he experiences God's speech in and beyond the Qur'an recital. He listens to revelation itself, flawless and matchless, spoken by God in clear Arabic without mistake and beyond translation into any other tongue. Standing in the presence of God, bowing and prostrating, he gives concrete expression to what it means to be Muslim, one who submits to Allah as his servant – the daily routine manifesting the Servant-of-God paradigm animating Islam at its core. The order of the five precise prayer times provides the daily rhythm for Muslim society, not unlike the hours ruling the day of the monk. It is as if the microcosm of monastic rule had been transposed on to the macrocosm of Muslim daily life by the routine of prayer, symbolizing the rule of divine law, *shari'a*, over Muslim society.

Ritual prayer hardened into legal duty and the daily routine of a body bent in prostration did not satisfy the thirst for knowledge and love of God cherished by the Sufis, the mystics of Islam, who set out to discover the divine word at the very dawn of creation. Until the Sufis, the decisive religious moment for humanity hinged on one single point, Abraham's awe-filled recognition of the one true nameless God. The Sufis pushed this moment back into pre-existence, when all human beings heard and understood God's self-revelation for the first time. Through a practice known as *dhikr*, anamnesis or recollection of God (which resembles the *mnēmē Theou* and hesychastic prayer of Eastern Christianity), the mystics return to their primaeval origin on the Day of Covenant, when all of humanity (symbolically enshrined in the prophetical ancestors as light particles or seeds) swore an oath of allegiance and witness to Allah as the one and only Lord. Through *dhikr*, understood as the active memory of God's first word, the mystics recall God's presence revealed within their heart and realize that the Lord of his servants alone can truly say, 'I am' (Ana) to the exclusion of any other and all else. Breaking through to eternity, they relive their primaeval moment with God, here and now, in the instant of ecstasy. Whether practised as individual prayer or communal ceremony, whether intimate colloquy or dance of the whirling dervish, *dhikr* discovers the roots of Abrahamic monotheism in the primaeval profession of God's oneness echoing in the hearts of the servants at the moment of mystical union with the divine.

2. Islamic time

The Sufi discovery of the pre-existential origin of all humanity on the Day of Covenant established a dimension of time that traced the present moment back to eternity in the past and balanced the eschatological thrust of the Qur'an from the present to eternity in the future, reached at the moment of the Day of Resurrection. The Sufis did not only look out to their ultimate destiny but anticipated it, here and now, in the light of certitude about the vision of God's face and the sounds of God's voice at the universal resurrection. In their prayer, they captured the sense of time that enlivens Islam and, by recollection and anticipation, drew it from its edges in pre- and post-existence into the moment of mystic experience. Sufi experience gave expression to an Islamic notion of time that is suspended between two days, Covenant and Resurrection, and resembles a parabola stretching from infinity to infinity, an arch anchored in eternity at its origin and end that reaches its apex in the moment of memory and certitude. (It neither forms a cycle of return nor describes a linear progression, rather it breaks open the circle of time and bends its arrow.) The moment itself is a time-atom in a finite, yet discontinuous galaxy of instants paralleling an atomistic concept of space existing only of mathematical points.

For Muslims, God is the Lord of the instant; what Allah has determined happens. The atomistic structure of time permeates a wide range of Muslim thought, including its legal and historical literature. The Qur'an overcame the pre-Islamic Arab notion of fate, impersonal time, with the idea of God as the Lord of time who fixes the terms of man's life and rules each of his moments. Islamic tradition further developed the Qur'anic notion by seeing time as a series of pre-determined events binding divine omnipotence to the certain occurrence of each instant in a person's life span. From the moment of birth to the stated term of death, individual existence falls under the decree of God which occurs instantaneously in time-atoms. In every instant God is creating the world anew; there are no intermediate causes and the universe is continually created from nothing. The Muslim theologians made atomism an instrument of divine omnipotence and providence and held that each moment within time is the direct creation of the eternally active God. Of itself, creation is discontinuous; it appears continuous only because of God's compassionate consistency. Most congenial to a vision of God acting instantaneously in the world as the sole true cause, atomism also proved closely akin to the Arabic language, which lacks genuine verbs for 'to be' and 'to become' and employs the verbal aspects of complete and incomplete, rather than the tenses of past, present and future.

3. Islamic thought

With atomism at the core of Islamic thought and language, a theological strategy was found to develop the servants' dependence on the one God and justify their direct confrontation with the Transcendent without recourse to a mediator. Islamic thought developed a strong sense of its vertical dimension of theology, which stresses trust in God, dependence on the Creator and obedience to God's will. It shortened, however, the horizontal dimension of anthropology, the autonomous self-realization of the human person, which the Christian sees rooted in incarnation and redemption. The disproportion of these two dimensions of Islamic thought that ascribed all power to God and severely limited the autonomy of human action became nowhere clearer than in the great dispute on free will and predetermination that preoccupied the Muslim inquisition in the ninth century (together with questions about the nature of the Qur'an). As the outcome of this debate Islam became firmly wedded to the view that God acts according to his foreknowledge of what he predetermined from eternity. He therefore controls all events and all human acts, which are his creation rather than the effect of human freedom of action, although human beings are responsible and accountable for everything they do.

V. Fundamentalism and prospects of modernity

Holding on to a mediaeval paradigm, dominated by ritual, law and an atomistic pattern of thought, contemporary Muslims find themselves forced to live on two tracks, one mediaeval, the other modern. The confrontation of these two conflicting outlooks was intuited by Salman Rushdie's *The Satanic Verses*. Published in 1988, this book is a fantastic amalgam written by an Indian Muslim living in Britain. It does violence to

Islamic sensibilities and levels an internal critique at Islam by way of a novel, harsher than any orientalist ever proposed. The book was banned and publicly burned by Muslims who saw it as blasphemy. The Ayatollah Khomeini issued a *fatwa*, a legal ruling, imposing the death sentence against the author, and huge sums of money were offered for his execution. The predicament of the story's Muslim hero facing the modern pluralistic world, used by the author to shake the foundations of a mediaeval Islamic world view, made the religious leaders of Islam explode in outrage and fear. For centuries, Islam had avoided critical examination of its sources and neglected radical reform of its mediaeval paradigm of thought and law. Now, it was hit with an imaginary and imaginative critique that wounded the religious nerve of Islam.

Today the Muslim world population is estimated to have reached almost one billion, one-fifth of humanity. Islam occupies the centre of the world. It stretches like a broad belt across the globe from the Atlantic to the Pacific, encircling both the 'haves' of the consumer North and the 'have-nots' of the disadvantaged South. It sits at the crossroads of America, Western Europe and Russia on one side and black Africa, India and East Asia on the other. Historically, Islam is also at the crossroads, destined to play a world role in politics and to become the most prominent world religion in the next century. Islam is not contained in any national culture; it is a universal force. Stretching from Morocco to Mindanao, it is built of five geographical blocks: the Muslims of black Africa, the Arab world, the Turco-Iranian lands (including Central Asia), the Muslims of South Asia and the inhabitants of the Indonesian archipelago. While Christianity has gone out to the nations, Islam has grown organically throughout history, expanding into new neighbouring territory without ever retreating (except in Spain, where it was expelled by force, and in the Balkans, where a similar process is at work in Bosnia today).

For Islam, the twentieth century began with the hope of secularism; it ends with the fear of fundamentalism. In 1924, Kemal Atatürk abolished the *shari'a* courts and secularized the then strongest Muslim empire on the globe, Ottoman Turkey. In 1979, Ayatollah Khomeini led the Iranian revolution to triumph, inspiring a variety of fundamentalist trends fermenting in the Muslim world. The world of Islam looks back nostalgically at the Middle Ages when its religion and culture seemed like identical twins and the Christian West studied at its feet. It senses with frustration that Western ideals of nationalism, socialism or capitalism, introduced into modern Muslim societies, have offered no true solutions to the manifold problems Islam faces in the technological world. With the slogans 'Islam is the solution' and 'Allah is the answer' (as the decals say), the fundamentalists pin their hopes on the utopia of a return to an idealized early Muslim community. 'Islam' is seen as the only principle that might revive the strength of Muslim society and lead it to a new (yet old) order in the Islamic state, with Islamic law as its rule. The test of fundamentalism will be its ability to organize a successful and stable Islamic state for tomorrow according to the blueprint of yesterday.

The most recent past has seen the Muslims of the diaspora grow into small, active minorities in America and Europe, sitting on the new frontier in the West. This Muslim diaspora has grown substantially in the last decades by immigration (as in England, France, Germany and Canada) and conversion (for example, the Black Muslims in the United States). Given greater intellectual freedom than in most Muslim nations, believers have gained wide access to advanced educational resources and acquired a certain distance from indigenous social pressures. Only the future can tell whether this Muslim diaspora will find the autonomy and creativity to sow the seeds of a genuine Islamic renewal in the pluralistic world. Unfortunately, the Christian minorities in Muslim countries have not experienced a similar measure of freedom. On the contrary, events in Egypt, Nigeria, Pakistan, Sudan and Turkey have shown their precarious situation as frequent subjects of human-rights violations.

Islam began with Muhammad's desire to bring God's message to the Arabs in their tongue. It was a message of reform, modelled on Abraham and anchored in witness to the one God. It also provided a common denominator for the conflicting views of Christian (and Judaeo-Christian) groups, uniting them under the Servant-of-God ideal of an uncompromising monotheism. By linking Abrahamic monotheism with the iconoclastically purified Arabian cult and clinging to its own holy book, Islam entered on the course of a separate religion. That separation was made firm when it wrote its own history not only in prayer but also in blood and so became stretched taut in a bow of tension between striving for God and struggle for dominion. The process of its growth from reform to religion was helped by the world of Christianity which dismissed it as just another heresy (e.g., John Damascene, died 749) and failed to hear its genuine call to reform in a wilderness of conflicting sects pushed to the fringes of Christendom. By establishing its own laws and ritual and by developing its own paradigm of time and pattern of atomistic thought, Islam defined its own parameters of a world religion. After a long history of confrontation along the Mediterranean in the Middle Ages, and with the collapse of colonial supremacy of the West in this century, the Muslim call to reform has caught up today with Christianity on global boundaries. Its new dimensions of challenge and growing conflict can no longer be neglected.

The Abrogation of Judaism and Christianity in Islam: A Christian Perspective

Jane Dammen McAuliffe

Ninety years ago in London the Society for Promoting Christian Knowledge published a volume by the Reverend W. St Clair Tisdall entitled, *A Manual of the Leading Muḥammadan Objections to Christianity*. Tisdall, a learned British scholar, cast the work as a dialogue between an imagined Muslim interlocutor and his Christian respondent, intending it to serve as a handbook for Christian missionaries. An unabashed piece of classical *apologia*, it is very much a product of its era, a time when Britain still controlled much of south Asia and the outbreak of World War I was a decade in the future. Yet Tisdall's little handbook, like this issue of *Concilium*, builds towards a consideration of the same issue, that most comprehensive challenge with which Islam confronts Judaism and Christianity, the claim that Muḥammad is the 'seal of the prophets' and that the revelation accorded him abrogates all previous ones.

Such continuity should not surprise, for what more sweeping charge can one religion address to another?[1] The history of Christian apologetics records countless replies to this Muslim challenge, replies, however, which do not always display a thorough understanding of the Muslim claim. Certainly, any contemporary Christian response should first demonstrate a clear comprehension of the Islamic conception of what Christians would call 'salvation history'. It should, in other words, begin with an empathetic attempt to see through Muslim eyes.

The grid which forms and filters that gaze is the Qur'ān, the verbatim compilation of God's revelations to his prophet Muḥammad. Before applying to this Qur'ānic source base, however, a cautionary remark is prompted by the present constraints of space. While the Qur'ān, like the Hebrew Bible and the New Testament, is a foundational religious scripture, it is by no means the only font of Muslim thought and practice. Like its biblical counterparts, the Qur'ān has generated a centuries-long exegetical endeavour and has fostered frequent renewal efforts within the tradition. To isolate but one segment or era of Islamic reflection, be it the formative Qur'ānic stage, a particular period within the mediaeval development of this tradition or the multi-faceted contemporary situation, risks truncating the richness and diversity of Islam and arbitrarily confining it to some predetermined perspective, whether past or present.

I. Moses and Jesus were Muslims

For Muslims, Islam is not simply God's final revelation but also God's first. Both cosmically and individually, the natal condition of human beings is that of submission *(islām)* to God. An important Qur'ānic passage (7,172) vividly depicts the primordial covenant which God forged with his creation: 'When your Lord brought forth their seed from the loins of the sons of Adam and made them testify on their own behalf, saying, "Am I not your Lord?", they said, "Most certainly; we have testified."' The verse closes with God's explanation that he had forged this covenant with humankind lest 'you say on the Day of Resurrection that "of this we were unaware."' If, as a species, humans are ontologically Muslim, they are also individually so. This condition, subsumed under the concept of *fiṭrah*, finds expression in a famous *ḥadīth* (saying) ascribed to Muḥammad: 'Every child is born a Muslim (*'alā al-fiṭrah*) but his father makes him a Jew, Christian or Magian/Zoroastrian.'[2] Like all humans, therefore, Moses and Jesus were Muslim. Further, as prophets, they were privileged with a special divine covenant (33,7): 'When We took their covenant *(mīthāq)* from the prophets, from you [Muḥammad] and from Noah, Abraham, Moses and Jesus, son of Mary, and We took from them a binding covenant.'[3]

God sent the prophets just named, and many others, to particular peoples so that they might remind their listeners of the primordial covenant and summon them to submission *(islām)*. While much of contemporary Judaism and Christianity operates within an understanding of prophetic 'inspiration', classical Islamic thought has functioned with what might be termed a 'doctrine of dictation'. In the Muslim concept of revelatory activity, the human filter is far more transparent. Prophets receive and transmit God's very words and Muslims revere Moses and Jesus, like their prophetic predecessors, as faithful conduits of God's invariant message to humankind. While there is a contextual aspect to God's inducement of the prophetic function, the Islamic notion of prophet-as-divine-mouthpiece is essentially atemporal. God's words, like his will, can never change, so that the message conveyed by Abraham or Moses or Jesus or Muḥammad has an inherent and inviolable continuity. Were it possible to recapture those earlier messages as originally proclaimed, Muslims believe that they would be perfectly consonant with the Qur'ān. To account for the evident inconsistency in their current redactions, Muslim apologists and theologians have developed a doctrine of scriptural corruption that is prefatory to the more sweeping assertion of abrogation.

II. The double charge of abrogation

The assertion of abrogation *(naskh)*[4] has both a circumscribed and a comprehensive connotation. In its more restricted sense, the charge constitutes a qualified *annulment* of both the Jewish and Christian scriptures. More broadly construed, it nullifies the continuing validity of those traditions themselves. Again, it is important to note that a very different understanding of scripture and of scriptural transmission undergirds these claims. It is also important to recognize that the Qur'ānic designation for the revelation accorded to Moses, the *Tawrat*, and for that accorded to Jesus, the *Injīl*, coincide with neither the Hebrew Bible nor the New Testament respectively. The *Tawrat* is roughly analogous to the Torah portion of the Hebrew Bible, while the *Injīl* (the term is an Arabic singular) is simply a kind of generic Gospel. (Even that characterization is misleading because as a genre, the Christian Gospels, which contain accounts of Jesus' words and deeds, are actually closer to the Muslim *ḥadīth*, the collected sayings and actions of Muḥammad.) Both are conceptualized as proto-Qur'āns, i.e., as compilations of God's direct verbal revelation to Moses and Jesus. Consequently, the reliability, or unreliability, of their subsequent transmission matters greatly. Judgment of their authenticity necessarily involves considerations of both content *(matn)* and conveyance *(isnād)*.

Muslims, therefore, ground the Qur'ānic *abrogation of Jewish and Christian scriptures* in their assessment of the latter *as textually and semantically corrupt*.[5] Simply put, the logic of this position is as follows: what Jews and Christians now recognize as their scriptures does not coincide with the Qur'ān, God's full and final revelation. Since God's word does not change, this lack of consonance must be consequent upon either deliberate or inadvertent alteration *(taḥrīf)* of the text and interpretation of these prior scriptures.[6] Muslim theologians and apologists, however, rarely present the charge of *taḥrīf* as a wholesale rejection of either the Hebrew Bible or the New Testament. Rather, they balance assertions of their textual and semantic corruption with the insistence that both scriptures announce the advent of Muḥammad and the success of his mission.

Nevertheless, for the most part the Jewish and Christian scriptures do not provide a reliable transmission of God's words to Moses and Jesus. Further, those prophets, like all prophets prior to Muḥammad, served the divine purpose in a limited and provisional manner. Only with the 'seal of the prophets', Muḥammad b. ʿAbdallāh, did God bring this prolonged process of revelation to complete fulfilment. While recognizing the value of earlier revelations in their original, uncorrupted form, and while acknowledging the time-bound validity of the religious practice which flowed from them, Islam operates with the inherent advantage of posteriority. As the self-confessed final revelation, the Qur'ān abrogates all previous scriptures. As the final revelatory codification of God's primordial and eternal will for humans. Islam abrogates all prior religions.

III. A retrospective reconsideration

If the foregoing represents an accurate, if very general, portrayal of the classical Muslim posture towards earlier religions, it also conveys a particular theological perspective and creates the context within which a Christian response can proceed. At least implicitly, this depiction acknowledges that God operates both through and beyond humanly designated religious traditions. Dogmatic and institutional boundaries do not confine the divine initiative. Consequently, a Christian can legitimately seek God's self-expression in its multiple historical and contemporary embodiments. Further, as they feel the force of Islam's challenge, Christians can reflect upon the effects of their own classical apologetic postures toward other religions. An obvious instance of this would be the Christian attitude toward Judaism.

Muslim scholars have always been quick to note that Islam's abrogation of Christianity mirrors the Christian abrogation of Judaism. Any Christian resentment at the Muslim assertion must surely be tempered with a concomitant recollection of how Christianity took the same advantage of its own position of posteriority. While it may be more accurate to say that Christianity see itself as the *fulfilment* of Judaism whereas Islam sees itself as the *restoration* of what Judaism and Christianity should have been, had they not suffered corruption, both are forms of abrogation. Greater sensitivity, therefore, to the alienation occasioned by Christian assertions of abrogation should surely be a consequence of struggling to respond to the Muslim charge. Similarly, Muslims may find in themselves a similar sensitivity as they face the challenge presented by post-Muḥammad movements such as that of the Bahāʾīs and the Aḥmadiyyah.

IV. The traditional response

Within the long history of Muslim-Christian polemic, the most persistent Christian response to the assertion of abrogation has been a straightforward rejection of the Muslim understanding of Christianity. Christians apologists have repeatedly insisted that the Qurʾānic and post-Qurʾānic comprehension of Christian doctrine is seriously flawed. The polemic itself centres upon three main issues: the reality of Jesus' crucifixion and death, the doctrine of the incarnation and the Christian understanding of God as trinity. For all three, the Qurʾānic account and its subsequent interpretation and elaboration stand at considerable variance with normative Christian self-understanding. For centuries, therefore, Christians have not been able to see themselves in the mirror of Muslim reflection. For equally as long, the theological debate engendered by these issues has deadlocked upon the assertion of Qurʾānic superiority. While this mutual theological reflection serves an important function, the Christian response should not stop there. By its very nature, religious polemic reinforces sectarian boundaries and fortifies the divisions between traditions. Yet through much closer contact, both professional and social, with those of other faiths, contemporary Christians are increasingly aware of the spiritual richness to be found in other traditions. Consequently many Christians are daily encouraged to appreciate the divine overtures which these traditions disclose.

V. Invitations to Christian self-assessment

Appreciative reflection upon the major elements of Muslim faith and practice can illuminate and enhance Christian life in manifold ways.[7] Islam, which means 'submitting oneself [to God]', exalts the majestic otherness of the divine. While certainly worshipping a merciful and compassionate God, it repudiates those theologies, Christian or otherwise, which attempt to cast God in a human image or which categorically presume to speak the divine word and will. A profound sense of reverence permeates the Muslim attitude towards God, a reverence physically expressed in the postures of daily prayer. The deep bow of the body, the head touching the ground, express human submission incarnate. A Christian remembers the powerful moment of prostration during the rites of ordination but also recalls how few are the liturgical demands made of the body. The month-long (Ramaḍān) withdrawal from all food, drink and sexual relations during the daylight hours focusses corporeal attention upon the Muslim's complete dependence on God. The contemporary observance of Lent falls far short of the rigour demanded by Ramaḍān. Perhaps Islam's more intensive and more expressive forms of body prayer can prompt Christians to a fuller appreciation of the divine embodiment in creation and incarnation.

While the doctrine of the incarnation remains a point of controversy between Muslims and Christians, Jesus as an esteemed model for emulation does not. The Qur'anic portrayal of Jesus, and of his mother Mary, is steeped in devotion. Islam and Christianity converge on the concept that humans can do God's will by imitating the actions of a sinless model.[8] Following the *sunnah*, or 'path', of Muḥammad provides the central focus of Muslim religious behaviour. Massive *ḥadīth* collections lavish extraordinary attention upon every detail of his speech and activity. Although the authenticity of particular *ḥadīths* has long been an object of both Muslim and Western scholarship, the functional importance of this totality, as a guide for Muslim behaviour, remains unassailable. While the Gospels provide an analogous repository of a community's devout recollection of its formative figure, Christians cannot help but admire the extraordinary energy which propelled *ḥadīth* collection for many generations of Muslims and the continuing vitality with which this record of his *sunnah* imbues Muḥammad's memory.

Attention to the Islamic *ummah* (community), the sisterhood and brotherhood of believers, offers Christians yet another opportunity for thoughtful self-assessment. The annual pilgrimage (*Ḥajj*) rituals in Mecca dramatically demonstrate the corporate embodiment of the Muslim sense of worldwide community. Many Christians, who are otherwise quite unfamiliar with Islamic values and practice, have been profoundly touched by the autobiographical account of the African-American leader, Malcolm X, who exulted in the spirit of fellowship which he felt within the Muslim community, particularly during the *Ḥajj* that he made in 1964.[9] A recent cinematic version of this autobiography has conveyed his experience to millions more and has reminded them of both the potent symbolism and the powerful reality of this expression of Muslim solidarity.

VI. From appreciation to mutual support

Attention has been drawn here to but a few aspects of the Islamic tradition which can elicit Christian appreciation and prompt an awareness of the dogmatically unfettered workings of the Spirit. But such appreciation should not be stillborn. Whether sparked by the New Testament's promise of the Spirit who 'will guide you to all truth' (John 16.13) or by the Qur'ān's injunction to 'Vie with one another for forgiveness from your Lord' (3.133), this sense of religious affinity can quickly move toward mutual support. Both Christians and Muslims strain against the confinements of secularity and seek ways to express their religious values in surroundings largely antithetical to such pursuits. Many live under political regimes which, whether nominally Muslim or Christian, pervert the religious principles which they ostensibly profess. Consequently, individuals within both traditions suffer the effects of religious repression and struggle to advance the intellectual conversation which each faith must continue with the thought worlds of modernity and postmodernity. Finally, no religious tradition can exempt itself from the challenges presented by global environmental problems. The universalistic claims which both Islam and Christianity advance need not preclude their collaboration in these and other areas. As Muslims and Christians deepen their mutual comprehension and enlarge their mutual appreciation, together they can generate fruitful systems of support and solidarity.

Notes

1. Many Muslims continue to react strongly against Bahā'ī assertions of this nature and those made by groups, such as the Ahmadiyyah, which question the finality of Muhammad's prophetic mission.

2. Muhammad Ismā'īl al-Bukhārī, *Sahpih*, Cairo 1968, VI, 143.

3. The Qur'anic category of prophet, which begins with Adam, includes figures not ordinarily subsumed under the biblical category.

4. *Naskh* also functions as a technical term with the Qur'anic exegetical sciences. For a fine recent study of this see John Burton, *The Sources of Islamic Law*, Edinburgh 1990.

5. The positions taken by classical Muslim scholars on this issue have ranged widely, with that of the Andalusian Abū Muhammad b. 'Alī b.Ḥazm (died 1064) being among the most rigorous and amply documented. For a recent study of the subject see H. Lazarus-Yafeh, *Intertwined Worlds*, Princeton 1992.

6. Historians of Islamic thought regularly note that this charge was initially levied with greater force against the Jewish scriptures but was later generalized to apply equally to the Christian.

7. For the Roman Catholic church the Vatican II declaration *Nostra aetate* constitutes an important advance in this direction. For a study of this declaration and its successive versions see M. Ruokanen, *The Catholic Doctrine of Non-Christian Religions*, Leiden 1992. An Arabic translation of the declaration may be found in *al-Wathā'īq al-Majma 'iyyah*, Antiyas, Lebanon 1984, 861–7.

8. The concept of prophetic impeccability (*'iṣmah*) has generated a considerable literature. A lengthy presentation of representative positions may be found in Fakhr al-Dīn al-Rāzī's (died 1210) *Kitāb al-arba 'īn*, Hyderabad 1934, or *'Iṣmat al-anbiyā'*, Cairo 1986, which have sections on Abraham, Moses, Jesus, Muhammad, etc.

9. Alex Haley (as told to), *The Autobiography of Malcolm X*, New York 1964.

IV · Perspectives on the Present and the Future

World Peace – World Religions – World Ethic

Hans Küng

Most commentators of our time agree that after the unexpected events of 1989 the world political situation as a whole has become more unstable, more uncertain. No one thought it possible that the world historical scene would change so rapidly: the collapse of the Soviet system, the reunification of Germany, the democratization of the former Eastern bloc states, the Gulf War, the civil war in former Yugoslavia. No one can as yet say definitively where all these developments are leading. But one thing seems certain: the collapse of Marxist socialism in 1989 and the break-up of the antagonistic military blocks is – if I see things correctly – a third chance for new world order, following those which were missed after the First World War in 1918 and the Second World War in 1945.

I. Three chances for a new world order: 1918 – 1945 – 1989

Chance 1: 1918. After the First World War, the 'League of Nations' was founded, on the instigation of the then American President Wilson (1920). This was based on the vision of the nations finally arriving at a shared, peaceful and just control of world affairs. But Europe and the world missed this first chance: above all with Fascism and National Socialism, but also with Communism and Japanese militarism, and following them with the Second World War, the Holocaust, the Gulag Archipelago and Hiroshima. Instead of a world order there was **world chaos.**

Chance 2: 1945. At that time there was another chance of such a new world order, and the 'United Nations' which was now founded was to help towards this. But this new attempt, too, proved divided. And it was above all the Stalinist Soviet Union which prevented a better order in Eastern Europe and elsewhere and dug its own grave by internal totalitarianism and external hegemonism. Instead of a world order there was a **division of the world**. Now to an unbridled capitalism with negative results above all in Latin America and Africa there was added a socialism which from the Elbe to Vladivostok led to an unprecedented enslaving of human beings and exploitation of nature – until it could go on no longer.

Chance 3: 1989. Now we have the third chance of what I would call a 'postmodern' world order. Politically, it presupposes the democratic state, and economically a market economy with both a social and ecological orientation (not to be confused with 'capitalism', which is neither social nor ecological), at least as it is affirmed in principle from Washington via Brussels to Moscow, even if it is far from being developed. But such a world order will not come into being without a new relationship between the nations. And who could have guessed that once again within Europe a war of unimaginable cruelty would be waged? Other regions, too, are far from being pacified. Is there a new **world disorder** instead of a new world order?

If we look at today's world, there is no getting round the terrifying fact that at present around thirty armed conflicts are going on. The UN is already overtaxed with thirteen peacekeeping missions under way. At present the UN numbers 184 member states (as compared with 51 in 1945). The unofficial estimate is that if Africa were also to be divided up by ethnic boundaries the number of 'sovereign states' could approach 450. But if smaller and smaller ethnic and religious units want to win the status of a 'sovereign state' for themselves, not only Africa, but also Europe from Spain to Russia, will be thrown into disorder by the splintering. The future will then be more insecure than ever. There will no longer be any question of stability if the units get smaller and smaller, the perspectives narrower and narrower, the pressures towards national damarcation more and more fanatical. Yugoslavia is a warning. And what has also been happening in Germany between Rostock, Solingen and Constance is a cruel warning of the need to rethink and to arrive at better rules for society in this one world and one humankind. But how?

II. No new world order without a world ethic

First of all, a **negative** statement: a new, better world order will **not** be introduced on the basis
– solely of diplomatic offensives, which all too often are addressed only to governments and not to peoples and which only too often are unable to guarantee the peace and stability of a region;
– simply of humanitarian help, which cannot replace political action;
– primarily of military interventions, the consequences of which tend more to be negative than positive;
– solely of 'international law', as long as this rests on the unlimited sovereignty of states and is focussed more on the rights of states than on the rights of peoples and individuals (human rights).

Then a **positive** statement: a new world order will ultimately be **brought in only on the basis of**
– more common visions, ideals, values, aims and criteria;
– a heightened global responsibility on the part of peoples and their leaders;
– a new binding and uniting ethic for all humankind, including states and those in power in them, which embraces cultures and religions. **No new world order without a new world ethic!**

Someone may object: given the war in Yugoslavia, where Orthodox Serbs, Catholic Croats and Muslim Bosnians are engaging in cruel and bloody slaughter; given the situation in the Middle East; given the tensions between Christian Armenians and Muslim Azerbijanis; between Hindus, Muslims and Sikhs in India; between Buddhist Singhalese and Hindu Tamils in Sri Lanka; and not least given the unresolved conflict in Northern Ireland between Catholics and Protestants, is it not crazy, in order to safeguard the future of this earth, to call for a world ethic to which the religions are to make a decisive contribution? My counter-question would be: when could such a demand be more urgent than today? At all events 'world ethic' is not a fair weather slogan, a luxury which might arouse academic interest or give one a good profile as a ceremonial speaker. It arises out of the bitter experiences of the past, the bloody crises of yesterday, in which the religions have often played a fatal role. But crisis means not only danger but also opportunity.

III. Not a single world culture or world religion

World politics, the world economy and the world financial system
play an essential part in determining our national and regional destiny.
Even in Switzerland people are slowly beginning to see that there are no
longer any national or regional islands of stability. And despite the
marked splintering of national and regional interests there is already such
a strong political, economic and financial **world network** that
economists are speaking of a **world society** and sociologists of a **world
civilization** (in the technical, economic and social sense): a world
society and world civilization as a coherent field of interaction in which all
are involved, either directly or indirectly.

But this world society and technological world civilization which is
coming into being in no way also means a single **world culture** (in the
spiritual – artistic – formative sense) or even a **world religion**. Rather,
world society and world civilization include a **multiplicity of cultures
and religions**, some of which even have new emphases. To hope for a
single world religion is an illusion; to be afraid of it is nonsense. The
multiplicity of religions, confessions and denominations, of religious
sects, groups and movements in today's world is still perplexing. They
form a complex phenomenon geographically, historically and culturally,
which cannot and must not be put under a single heading.

But if we do not want to reduce this overcomplexity which has grown
up down the centuries and want to adopt an approach which is not only
regional or national but **world-historical and world-wide** and in this
sense **planetary;** if, given the present complexity which is also, indeed
particularly, to be found in matters of religion, we are seeking a new
orientation also and particularly in matters of religion, then in view of
what Wilfrid Cantwell Smith has called the 'one religious history of
humankind' we will do best to keep to the great religious river systems of
the **high religions** which still exist today, and which have also inundated
the nature religions of Africa, America and Oceania. If we look at the
world today, seeing our globe as it were from a satellite, in the cultural
landscape of this earth at present we can distinguish **three great
religious river systems** with their areas of entry, **transcending
individuals, nations and cultures,** and all of which have their own
genesis and morphology:

  • the religions of **Semitic** origin: these have a **prophetic** character,
  always begin from a **contrast** between God and human beings, and are
  predominantly marked by religious confrontation: Judaism, Christianity and Islam;

- the religions of **Indian** origin: they primarily have a basically mystical tone, tending towards **union**, and are characterized more by religious **inwardness**: the early Indian religion of the Upanishads, Buddhism and Hinduism;
- the religions of the **Chinese** tradition: these are stamped by wisdom and are fundamentally characterized by harmony: Confucianism and Taoism.

Older, stronger and more constant than many dynasties and empires, these great religous systems have modelled the cultural landscape of this globe over the millennia. In an incessant rhythm of change, sporadically new mountain chains and high plateaus have thrust themselves up on the different continents, but the great **rivers**, older, stronger and more constant, have kept making ever-new cuts in the rising landscape. Similarly, in our cultural landscape ever-new social systems, states and ruling houses have arisen, but the great old rivers of the **religions** have been able – despite all the rises and falls – to maintain themselves with a few adaptations and deviations and have shaped the features of the cultural landscape in a new way. Simply because of that, because of the far-reaching ways in which cultures have been shaped by religions, it would make no sense to speak of a single world culture or world religion or even to attempt to.

And yet, there are **features which the religions have in common**. Just as the natural river systems of this earth and the landscapes shaped by them are extremely different, but the rivers and streams of the different continents all have similar profiles and patterns of flow, obey similar laws, cut clefts in the hills, wind in the plains and inexorably seek a way to the sea, so too it is with the religious river systems of this earth. Although they are extremely different, in many respects they display similar profiles, regularities and effects. Confusingly different though religions all are, they are all messages of salvation which all respond to similar **basic human questions**, to the eternal questions of love and sorrow, guilt and atonement, life and death. Where does the world and its order come from? Why are we born and why must we die? What determines the destiny of the individual and of humankind? What is the basis of moral awareness and of the presence of ethical norms? And over and above their interpretation of the world, all also offer similar **ways of salvation**: ways out of the distress, suffering and guilt of being, pointers towards meaningful and responsible action in this life – towards a permanent, lasting eternal salvation, redemption from all suffering, from guilt and death.

Now all this means that even those who reject the religions (and in my book *Does God Exist?* I have subjected all the arguments of the modern criticism of religion to a thorough examination) will have to take them seriously as a fundamental social and existential reality; they all have to do with meaning and meaninglessness in life, with human freedom and slavery, with justice and the oppression of peoples, with war and peace in history and the present.

IV. Taking the religious dimension seriously

There is no doubt about it: any **religion** is **ambivalent** as a human phenomenon – as ambivalent as art or music, which also have been and are massively misused. Sociologically, religions too are systems of power concerned for stabilization and the extension of power. They have a high potential for conflict. But they also have an often overlooked potential for peace. Religion can stir things up, certainly, but it can also calm them down. **Religion can motivate, foment and prolong wars,** but it can also **prevent wars and shorten them.**

The foundations for the peace between France, Germany and Italy were laid by convinced Christians (and Catholics): Charles de Gaulle, Konrad Adenauer, Robert Schumann, Alcide de Gasperi.

Peace between Germany and Poland was prepared for by a memorandum drafted by the Protestant Church (the Evangelical Church of Germany).

Peaceful revolutions in Poland, East Germany, Czechoslovakia and also in South Africa and the Philippines have shown that religion can also serve to bring about peace.

Here I would like to say quite clearly that the purely strategic, economic and political aspects of such crises must not be allowed to overshadow their social, moral and religious aspects. Here is just one **example**, from what used to be **Yugoslavia**.

Anyone who is not blind to history will have noticed that the modern state frontiers in Eastern Europe seem pale in comparison with the age-old frontiers which were once drawn by religions and confessions: between Armenia and Azerbijan, between Georgia and Russia, the Ukraine and Russia, and similarly also between the different peoples in Yugoslavia. It is possible to understand the complexity of the problems in Yugoslavia only if one knows that for a thousand years – basically since the division between Western and Eastern Rome – two different religions have been meeting in the middle of Yugoslavia: the Eastern Byzantine paradigm with Serbia and the Roman Catholic paradigm with Croatia. Catholic Croats could get on better with Muslims than with Orthodox fellow Christians . . . In addition, there are the problems of the five-hundred year occupation of Serbian territory by the Turks (since the defeat at Kosovo polje in 1389), which among the Serbs produced the ideology of a lasting suffering and endurance which very often does not (or does not any longer) correspond to reality.

Now the Serbs, Croats and Bosnians (the only indigenous Muslims in Europe) are all southern Slavs. For centuries Serbs have lived among Croats, originally recruited against the Turks, as ethnic cousins. And so today the three groups are highly mixed in the state territory of what once was Yugoslavia, most of all in Bosnia. So it was wrong after 1989 first of all to defend a single uniform Yugoslav state (Phase 1 of the EC and US policy), but also wrong then to go to the opposite extreme and split the whole of Yugoslavia into national states (Phase 2, especially German and then also EC and US policy). A confederation (with cantons or whatever) would have been the right course to take from the beginning, and not just now, when it is too late.

Will there ever be peace in such a region if the religious dimension of the conflict is not taken seriously? In the present conflict my sympathies were first of all with Croatia (not because it was Catholic but because it had been attacked) and then above all with the Muslims. But may I as a Catholic theologian keep silent about the fact that the Catholic Croatian Ustasha state under the Nazi protectorate killed tens of thousands (some say hundreds of thousands) of Serbs without a single protest at the time from Archbishop Stepinac of Zagreb or Pope Pius XII, both of whom were very well informed? But truly, the Orthodox Serbs also have their overloaded list of guilty actions.

Over forty years both churches could have found time to sort out the situation, concede guilt, ask for forgiveness, and prepare for a political peace. The World Council of Churches, often more concerned with the world than the churches, certainly meant well when in the middle of the civil war it brought together bishops from both sides, though their ecumenical discourses ended in unecumenical accusations. Indeed whether one speaks today with a Serb or a Croat, each talks about the crimes of the other side and says nothing about the crimes of his own side – just like the Germans and French of old. Will Serbs and Croats need yet another war of revenge before they become aware that such thought and policy dominated by revenge will never lead to peace but always only to new destruction? If a cease-fire should finally be achieved, will there still be no bishops or theologians who could begin to talk to one another in an understanding way? Self-critical recollection is unavoidable.

My basic question is: must these **religions** inevitably be engaged in conflict and strife? Peace (*shalom, salam, eirene, pax*) is a main feature of their programmes. Their first task at this time must be to **make peace among themselves,** in order with all the means which the media offer:
– to clear up misunderstandings;
– to work through traumatic memories;
– to dissolve stereotyped images of enemies;
– to come to terms with the conflicts of guilt socially and as individuals;
– to break down hatred and destructiveness;
– to reflect on what they have in common. Are the members of the different religions aware of the ethos they have in common – despite their great 'dogmatic' differences? Not at all.

V. The need for a minimal consensus on ethics

First of all, understanding among the religions does not require believers to line up against unbelievers. The Roman campaign for re-Catholicization, especially in Eastern Europe, euphemistically called re-evangelization, only leads to a re-opening of the old war graves: we do not need another division of society and political parties into clerical and anti-clerical (as for example in Poland). The project of a world ethic, a global ethic, calls rather for an **alliance of believers and non-believers** over a new common basic ethic.

Secondly, the religions without doubt have a special function and responsibility when it comes to binding criteria and personal basic convictions. What unites all the great **religions** needs to be worked out carefully and in detail on the basis of the sources – a significant and enjoyable task for the scholars of the different religions which is still in its beginnings, but has aroused much interest amazingly quickly and has produced a first result.

At a more fundamental level I would ask: what can religions contribute to the furthering of an ethic, **despite their very different systems of dogmas and symbols**, which distinguishes them from philosophy, political pragmatism, international organizations, philanthropic concerns of all kinds? Granted, in the past religions have always absolutized their traditions, fixed mysterious dogmas and ritual prescriptions and set themselves apart from any others. Yet where they want to, they can present fundamental **maxims of elementary humanity** with quite a different authority and power of conviction from that of politicians, lawyers and philosophers.

VI. A supreme norm of conscience and a leading figure

Granted, religions were and always are tempted to lose themselves in an infinite jungle of commandments and prescriptions, canons and paragraphs. Yet where they want to, they can demonstrate, with quite different authority from any philosophy, that the application of their norms does not apply to individual cases but is categorical. Religions can give men and women a **supreme norm of conscience,** that **categorical imperative** which is still important for today's society, which imposes an obligation at quite a different depth and on quite a different foundation. For all the great religions call for the observance of something like a **'Golden Rule'** – which is not just a hypothetical and conditional norm but one that is a categorical, apodeictic and unconditional norm – one that is quite practicable in the highly complex situation in which individuals or groups must often act.

This Golden Rule is already attested in **Confucius**: 'What you yourself do not want, do not do to another person' (Confucius, c.551–489 BCE); and also in **Judaism** (in a negative formulation): 'Do not do to others what you would not want them to do to you' (Rabbi Hillel, 60 BCE to 10 CE); and finally also in the **Sermon on the Mount** (in a positive formulation): 'Whatever you want people to do to you, do also to them.'

This Golden Rule could be a safeguard against a **crude ethics of success** which is not an ethic at all; it does not need to be understood as a pure dispositional ethic which does not perceive realities, but could become the centre of an **ethics of responsibility** (the term used by Max Weber and Hans Jonas), which always reflects on the consequences of what we do and allow.

The reference to Confucius and Jesus of Nazareth also already indicates something else: unlike philosophies, religions do not just offer abstract models of life. They can refer to specific individuals who have already gone that way, what Karl Jaspers calls 'normative people'. So the **normative leading figures** in the world religions are of the utmost significance: Buddha, Jesus of Nazareth, Con-fu-tse, Lao-tse or Muhammad. It makes a crucial difference whether one pontificates to people about a new form of life in the abstract or whether one can introduce them to such a form of life by means of a compelling concrete model: as followers of Buddha, Jesus Christ, Con-fu-tse, Lao-tse or the Prophet

Muhammad. For me as a Christian – to speak quite plainly here – Jesus Christ is and remains the way, the truth and the life (that is as it were my internal perspective), but (and this is at the same time my external perspective) I cannot avoid noting that 'the way, the truth and the life' is for believing Jews the Torah, for Muslims the Qur'an and for other religions someone or something else.

VII. The process of forming an awareness of a world ethic

But is the working out of such an ethic realistic? Is it perhaps just the undertaking of a few Western intellectuals who once again want to 'export' their project? No, the call for a world ethic is not a matter of 'exporting' of a model, an artificial 'globalization' or the 'idea of universality' as opposed to the 'idea of regionality'. Here we have neither a radical universalism which takes no note of the actual plurality in our world, nor a radical relativism, which does not contribute towards the common life of different groups but to what Wolfgang Huber calls a 'relative universality', which despite all cultural and religious differences recognizes some principles which transcend culture and religion. Indeed, to be more precise, it is a matter of **becoming aware of what culture and religions already have in common:** the formation of an awareness and hence a change of awareness in the sphere of ethics of the kind that has come about in, say, ecology or disarmament.

But is there even the slightest sign that anything is actually happening? I am happy to be able to report the following. At the centenary celebration of the Parliament of the World's Religions in Chicago at the beginning of September 1993, a 'Declaration towards a Global Ethic' was presented which I had the honour and the toil of working out; it was accepted by the vast majority of the delegates and in the end ceremonially promulgated. For the first time in the history of world religions this Parliament undertook to formulate a basic consensus over binding values, irrevocable criteria and basic personal attitudes. Granted, such a declaration will not change the world overnight, but it will encourage all those who are already committed to it and put to shame those who tend rather ironically to ridicule, to dismiss or from confessional egoism declare impossible anything that religions may have in common.

The significance of the 'Declaration towards a Global Ethic' can be illustrated at one point in particular in the context of Islam. For the 'four irrevocable directives' which are elucidated in this declaration include a 'commitment to a culture of non-violence and respect for life'. There was serious discussion of this point during the Parliament. For specifically in view of the desperate situation of the Muslims in Bosnia, too little emphasis seemed to be placed here on the right to self-defence (which is also affirmed by the United Nations Charter). However, on closer reading these fears proved to be ungrounded. For the Declaration deliberately took a middle way which was capable of achieving a consensus: between a 'Realpolitik' of the use of violence to resolve conflicts and an unrealistic unconditional pacifism which – when confronted with devastation, expulsion, violence, death, mass murder – unconditionally renounces the use of violence. The **right to self-defence** to which the Muslims attach importance is thus clearly affirmed both for the individual and the collective. But within the framework of a culture of non-violence it applies only *in extremis*, when non-violent resistance is meaningless. In the face of brutality, barbarism and genocide, self-defence has to be allowed. No further holocaust of any people whatsoever can simply be accepted in a pacifist way. On the other hand, no simple formula of legitimation can be offered for military intervention of any kind; no 'just wars' in the service of all too evident economic, political and military interests are to be justified in this way.

VIII. Towards a culture of non-violence

This is what the Global Ethic Declaration says about non-violence:

Numberless women and men of all regions and religions strive to lead lives not determined by egoism but by commitment to their fellow humans and to the world around them. Nevertheless, all over the world we find endless hatred, envy, jealousy and violence, not only between individuals but also between social and ethnic groups, between classes, races, nations, and religions. The use of violence, drug trafficking and organized crime, often equipped with new technical possibilities, has reached global proportions. Many places are still ruled by terror 'from above'; dictators oppress their own people, and institutional violence is widespread. Even in some countries where laws exist to protect individual freedoms, prisoners are tortured, men and women are mutilated, hostages are killed.

(a) In the great ancient religious and ethical traditions of humankind we find the directive: **You shall not kill!** *Or in positive terms:* **Have respect for life!** *Let us reflect anew on the consequences of this ancient directive: all people have a right to life, safety and the free development of personality in so far as they do not injure the rights of others. No one has the right physically or psychically to torture, injure, much less kill, any*

other human being. And no people, no state, no race, no religion has the right to hate, to discriminate against, to 'cleanse', to exile, much less to liquidate a 'foreign' minority which is different in behaviour or holds different beliefs.

(b) Of course, wherever there are humans there will be conflicts. Such conflicts, however, should be resolved without violence within a framework of justice. This is true for states as well as for individuals. Persons who hold political power must work within this framework of a just order and commit themselves to the most non-violent, peaceful solutions possible. And they should work for this within an international order of peace which itself has need of protection and defence against perpetrators of violence. Armament is a mistaken path; disarmament is the commandment of the times. Let no one be deceived; There is no survival for humanity without global peace!

(c) Young people must learn at home and in school that violence may not be a means of settling differences with others. Only thus can a **culture of non-violence** *be created.*

(d) A human person is infinitely precious and must be unconditionally protected. But likewise **the lives of animals and plants** *which inhabit this planet with us deserve protection, preservation, and care. Limitless exploitation of the natural foundations of life, ruthless destruction of the biosphere, and militarization of the cosmos are all outrages. As human beings we have a special responsibility – especially with a view to future generations – for Earth and the cosmos, for the air, water, and soil. We are all* **intertwined together** *in this cosmos and we are all dependent on each other. Each one of us depends on the welfare of all. Therefore the dominance of humanity over nature and the cosmos must not be encouraged. Instead, we must cultivate living in harmony with nature and the cosmos.*

(e) To be authentically human in the spirit of our great religious and ethical traditions means that in public as well as in private life we must be concerned for others and ready to help. We must never be ruthless and brutal. Every people, every race, every religion must show tolerance and respect – indeed high appreciation – for every other. Minorities need protection and support, whether they be racial, ethnic, or religious.

I am convinced that the new world order will only be a better order if as a result there we have a pluralistic world society characterized by partnership, which encourages peace and is nature-friendly and ecumenical. That is why even now many people are committing themselves on the basis of their religious or human convictions to a common world ethic and are calling all people of good will to contribute to a change of awareness in matters of ethics.

Translated by John Bowden

There is a commentary on the Declaration in *A Global Ethic. The Declaration of the Parliament of the World's Religions*, ed. Hans Küng and Karl-Josef Kuschel, London and New York 1993. Editions in other languages are available or in preparation.

Documentation

Universal Islamic Declaration of Human Rights

This Declaration of Human Rights *is the second fundamental document proclaimed by the Islamic Council to mark the beginning of the 15th Century of the Islamic Era, the first being the* Universal Islamic Declaration *announced at the International Conference on The Prophet Muhammad (peace and blessings be upon him) and his Message, held in London from 12 to 15 April 1980.*

The Universal Islamic Declaration of Human Rights *is based on the Qur'an and the Sunnah and has been compiled by eminent Muslim scholars, jurists and representatives of Islamic movements and thought. May God reward then all for their efforts and guide us along the right path.*

Preamble

WHEREAS the age-old human aspiration for a just world order wherein people could live, develop and prosper in an environment free from fear, oppression, exploitation and deprivation, remains largely unfulfilled;

WHEREAS the Divine Mercy unto mankind reflected in its having been endowed with super-abundant economic sustenance is being wasted, or unfairly or unjustly withheld from the inhabitants of the earth;

WHEREAS Allah (God) has given mankind through His revelations in the Holy Qur'an and the Sunnah of His Blessed Prophet Muhammad an abiding legal and moral framework within which to establish and regulate human institutions and relationships;

WHEREAS the human rights decreed by the Divine Law aim at conferring dignity and honour on mankind and are designed to eliminate oppression and injustice;

WHEREAS by virtue of their Divine source and sanction these rights can neither be curtailed, abrogated or disregarded by authorities, assemblies or other institutions, nor can they be surrendered or alienated;

Therefore we, as Muslims, who believe

a) in God, the Beneficent and Merciful, the Creator, the Sustainer, the Sovereign, the sole Guide of mankind and the Source of all Law;

b) in the Vicegerency (Khilafah) of man who has been created to fulfil the Will of God on earth;

c) in the wisdom of Divine guidance brought by the Prophets, whose mission found its culmination in the final Divine message that was conveyed by the Prophet Muhammad (Peace be upon him) to all mankind;

d) that rationality by itself without the light of revelation from God can neither be a sure guide in the affairs of mankind nor provide spiritual nourishment to the human soul, and, knowing that the teachings of Islam represent the quintessence of Divine guidance in its final and perfect form, feel duty-bound to remind man of the high status and dignity bestowed on him by God;

e) in inviting all mankind to the message of Islam;

f) that by the terms of our primeval covenant with God our duties and obligations have priority over our rights, and that each one of us is under a bounden duty to spread the teachings of Islam by word, deed, and indeed in all gentle ways, and to make them effective not only in our individual lives but also in the society around us;

g) in our obligation to establish an Islamic order:

   i) wherein all human beings shall be equal and none shall enjoy a privilege or suffer a disadvantage or discrimination by reason of race, colour, sex, origin or language;

ii) wherein all human beings are born free;

iii) wherein slavery and forced labour are abhorred;

iv) wherein conditions shall be established such that the institution of family shall be preserved, protected and honoured as the basis of all social life;

v) wherein the rulers and the ruled alike are subject to, and equal before, the Law;

vi) wherein obedience shall be rendered only to those commands that are in consonance with the Law;

vii) wherein all worldly power shall be considered as a sacred trust, to be exercised within the limits prescribed by the Law and in a manner approved by it, and with due regard for the priorities fixed by it;

viii) wherein all economic resources shall be treated as Divine blessings bestowed upon mankind, to be enjoyed by all in accordance with the rules and the values set out in the Qur'an and the Sunnah;

ix) wherein all public affairs shall be determined and conducted, and the authority to administer them shall be exercised after mutual consultation (*Shura*) between the believers qualified to contribute to a decision which would accord well with the Law and the public good;

x) wherein everyone shall undertake obligations proportionate to his capacity and shall be held responsible pro rata for his deeds;

xi) wherein everyone shall, in case of an infringement of his rights, be assured of appropriate remedial measures in accordance with the Law;

xii) wherein no one shall be deprived of the rights assured to him by the Law except by its authority and to the extent permitted by it;

xiii) wherein every individual shall have the right to bring legal action against anyone who commits a crime against society as a whole or against any of its members;

xiv) wherein every effort shall be made to

    (a) secure unto mankind deliverance from every type of exploitation, injustice and oppression,

(b) ensure to everyone security, dignity and liberty in terms set out and by methods approved and within the limits set by the Law;

Do hereby, as servants of Allah and as members of the Universal Brotherhood of Islam, at the beginning of the Fifteenth Century of the Islamic Era, affirm our commitment to uphold the following inviolable and inalienable human rights that we consider are enjoined by Islam.

I   Right to Life

a) Human life is sacred and inviolable and every effort shall be made to protect it. In particular no one shall be exposed to injury or death, except under the authority of the Law.

b) Just as in life, so also after death, the sanctity of a person's body shall be inviolable. It is the obligation of believers to see that a deceased person's body is handled with due solemnity.

II   Right to Freedom

a) Man is born free. No inroads shall be made on his right to liberty except under the authority and in due process of the Law.

b) Every individual and every people has the inalienable right to freedom in all its forms – physical, cultural, economic and political – and shall be entitled to struggle by all available means against any infringement or abrogation of this right; and every oppressed individual or people has a legitimate claim to the support of other individuals and/or peoples in such a struggle.

III   Right to Equality and Prohibition Against Impermissible Discrimination

a) All persons are equal before the Law and are entitled to equal opportunities and protection of the Law.

b) All persons shall be entitled to equal wage for equal work.

c) No person shall be denied the opportunity to work or be discriminated against in any manner or exposed to greater physical risk by reason of religious belief, colour, race, origin, sex or language.

IV   *Right to Justice*

a) Every person has the right to be treated in accordance with the Law, and only in accordance with the Law.

b) Every person has not only the right but also the obligation to protest against injustice; to recourse to remedies provided by the Law in respect of any unwarranted personal injury or loss; to self-defence against any charges that are preferred against him and to obtain fair adjudication before an independent judicial tribunal in any dispute with public authorities or any other person.

c) It is the right and duty of every person to defend the rights of any other person and the community in general (*Hisbah*).

d) No person shall be discriminated against while seeking to defend private and public rights.

e) It is the right and duty of every Muslim to refuse to obey any command which is contrary to the Law, no matter by whom it may be issued.

V   *Right to Fair Trial*

a) No person shall be adjudged guilty of an offence and made liable to punishment except after proof of his guilt before an independent judicial tribunal.

b) No person shall be adjudged guilty except after a fair trial and after reasonable opportunity for defence has been provided to him.

c) Punishment shall be awarded in accordance with the Law, in proportion to the seriousness of the offence and with due consideration of the circumstances under which it was committed.

d) No act shall be considered a crime unless it is stipulated as such in the clear wording of the Law.

e) Every individual is responsible for his actions. Responsibility for a crime cannot be vicariously extended to other members of his family or group, who are not otherwise directly or indirectly involved in the commission of the crime in question.

VI   *Right to Protection Against Abuse of Power*

Every person has the right to protection against harassment by official agencies. He is not liable to account for himself except for making a defence to the charges made against him or where he is found in a situation wherein a question regarding suspicion of his involvement in a crime could be *reasonably* raised.

VII   Right to Protection Against Torture

No person shall be subjected to torture in mind or body, or degraded, or threatened with injury either to himself or to anyone related to or held dear by him, or forcibly made to confess to the commission of a crime, or forced to consent to an act which is injurious to his interests.

VIII   Right to Protection of Honour and Reputation

Every person has the right to protect his honour and reputation against calumnies, groundless charges or deliberate attempts at defamation and blackmail.

IX   Right to Asylum

a) Every persecuted or oppressed person has the right to seek refuge and asylum. This right is guaranteed to every human being irrespective of race, religion, colour and sex.

b) Al Masjid Al Haram (the sacred house of Allah) in Mecca is a sanctuary for all Muslims.

X   Rights of Minorities

a) The Qur'anic principle 'There is no compulsion in religion' shall govern the religious rights of non-Muslim minorities.

b) In a Muslim country religious minorities shall have the choice to be governed in respect of their civil and personal matters by Islamic Law, or by their own laws.

XI   Right and Obligation to Participate in the Conduct and Management of Public Affairs

a) Subject to the Law, every individual in the community (*Ummah*) is entitled to assume public office.

b) Process of free consultation (*Shura*) is the basis of the administrative relationship between the government and the people. People also have the right to choose and remove their rulers in accordance with this principle.

XII   Right to Freedom of Belief, Thought and Speech

a) Every person has the right to express his thoughts and beliefs so long as he remains within the limits prescribed by the Law. No one, however, is entitled to disseminate falsehood or to circulate reports which may outrage public decency, or to indulge in slander, innuendo or to cast defamatory aspersions on other persons.

b) Pursuit of knowledge and search after truth is not only a right but a duty of every Muslim.

c) It is the right and duty of every Muslim to protest and strive (within the limits set out by the Law) against oppression even if it involves challenging the highest authority in the state.

d) There shall be no bar on the dissemination of information provided it does not endanger the security of the society or the state and is confined within the limits imposed by the Law.

e) No one shall hold in contempt or ridicule the religious beliefs of others or incite public hostility against them; respect for the religious feelings of others is obligatory on all Muslims.

XIII   Right to Freedom of Religion

Every person has the right to freedom of conscience and worship in accordance with his religious beliefs.

XIV   Right to Free Association

a) Every person is entitled to participate individually and collectively in the religious, social, cultural and political life of his community and to establish institutions and agencies meant to enjoin what is right (*ma'roof*) and to prevent what is wrong (*munkar*).

b) Every person is entitled to strive for the establishment of institutions whereunder an enjoyment of these rights would be made possible. Collectively, the community is obliged to establish conditions so as to allow its members full development of their personalities.

XV   The Economic Order and the Rights Evolving Therefrom

a) In their economic pursuits, all persons are entitled to the full benefits of nature and all its resources. These are blessings bestowed by God for the benefit of mankind as a whole.

b) All human beings are entitled to earn their living according to the Law.

c) Every person is entitled to own property individually or in association with others. State ownership of certain economic resources in the public interest is legitimate.

d) The poor have the right to a prescribed share in the wealth of the rich, as fixed by Zakah, levied and collected in accordance with the Law.

e) All means of production shall be utilized in the interest of the community (*Ummah*) as a whole, and may not be neglected or misused.

f) In order to promote the development of a balanced economy and to protect society from exploitation, Islamic Law forbids monopolies, unreasonable restrictive trade practices, usury, the use of coercion in the making of contracts and the publication of misleading advertisements.

g) All economic activities are permitted provided they are not detrimental to the interests of the community (*Ummah*) and do not violate Islamic laws and values.

XVI   Right to Protection of Property

No property may be expropriated except in the public interest and on payment of fair and adequate compensation.

XVII   Status and Dignity of Workers

Islam honours work and the worker and enjoins Muslims not only to treat the worker justly but also generously. He is not only to be paid his earned wages promptly, but is also entitled to adequate rest and leisure.

XVIII   Right to Social Security

Every person has the right to food, shelter, clothing, education and medical care consistent with the resources of the community. This obligation of the community extends in particular to all individuals who cannot take care of themselves due to some temporary or permanent disability.

XIX   Right to Found a Family and Related Matters

a) Every person is entitled to marry, to found a family and to bring up children in conformity with his religion, traditions and culture. Every spouse is entitled to such rights and privileges and carries such obligations as are stipulated by the Law.

b) Each of the partners in a marriage is entitled to respect and consideration from the other.

c) Every husband is obligated to maintain his wife and children according to his means.

d) Every child has the right to be maintained and properly brought up by its parents, it being forbidden that children are made to work at an early age or that any burden is put on them which would arrest or harm their natural development.

e) If parents are for some reason unable to discharge their obligations towards a child it becomes the responsiblity of the community to fulfil these obligations at public expense.

f) Every person is entitled to material support, as well as care and protection, from his family during his childhood, old age or incapacity. Parents are entitled to material support as well as care and protection from their children.

g) Motherhood is entitled to special respect, care and assistance on the part of the family and the public organs of the community (*Ummah*).

g) Within the family, men and women are to share in their obligations and responsibilities according to their sex, their natural endowments, talents and inclinations, bearing in mind their common responsibilities toward their progeny and their relatives.

i) No person may be married against his or her will, or lose or suffer dimunition of legal personality on account of marriage.

XX   *Rights of Married Women*

Every married woman is entitled to:

a) live in the house in which her husband lives;

b) receive the means necessary for maintaining a standard of living which is not inferior to that of her spouse, and, in the event of divorce, receive during the statutory period of waiting (*Iddah*) means of maintenance commensurate with her husband's resources, for herself as well as for the children she nurses or keeps, irrespective of her own financial status, earnings, or property that she may hold in her own right;

c) seek and obtain dissolution of marriage (*Khul'a*) in accordance with the terms of the Law. This right is in addition to her right to seek divorce through the courts.

d) inherit from her husband, her parents, her children and other relatives according to the Law.

e) strict confidentiality from her spouse, or ex-spouse if divorced, with regard to any information that he may have obtained about her, the disclosure of which could prove detrimental to her interests. A similar responsibility rests upon her in respect of her spouse or ex-spouse.

XXI   Right to Education

a) Every person is entitled to receive education in accordance with his natural capabilites.

b) Every person is entitled to a free choice of profession and career and to the opportunity for the full development of his natural endowments.

XXII   Right of Privacy

Every person is entitled to the protection of his privacy.

XXIII   Right to Freedom of Movement and Residence

a) In view of the fact that the World of Islam is veritably *Ummah Islamia*, every Muslim shall have the right to freely move in and out of any Muslim country.

b) No one shall be forced to leave the country of his residence, or be arbitrarily deported therefrom, without recourse to due process of Law.

Explanatory Notes

1 In the above formulation of Human Rights, unless the context provides otherwise:

a) the term 'person' refers to both the male and female sexes.

b) the term 'Law' denotes the *Shari'ah*, i.e. the totality of ordinances derived from the Qur'an and the Sunnah and any other laws that are deduced from these two sources by methods considered valid in Islamic jurisprudence.

2 Each one of the Human Rights ennunciated in this Declaration carries a corresponding duty.

3 In the exercise and enjoyment of the rights referred to above every person shall be subject only to such limitations as are enjoined by the Law for the purpose of securing the due recognition of, and respect for, the rights and the freedom of others and of meeting the just require-ments of morality, public order and the general welfare of the Community (*Ummah*).

4 The Arabic text of this *Declaration* is the original.

A New Document from the Papal Biblical Commission on 'The Interpretation of the Bible in the Church'

1993 marked the centenary of Leo XIII's encyclical *Providentissimus Deus*, and fifty years ago Pius XII published the encyclical *Divino afflante Spiritu*. Both documents dealt with the Catholic interpretation of Holy Scripture in the light of the biblical criticism of the time. They exercised great influence, the second – around three decades after the tragic Modernist dispute – more than the former. Together they paved the way for the integration of literary-historical exegesis into Catholic theology. Towards a rethinking of these encyclicals, the Papal Biblical Commission has issued a new document, 'L'interprétation de la Bible dans l'Église' (published in *La Documentation Catholique* 91, 1994, 13–44 and *Biblica* 74, 1993, 451–528). However, the anniversaries were not the only occasion for it. According to the accompanying letter by Cardinal Ratzinger, exegesis in the thirty years after *Dei Verbum*, the Vatican II document which endorsed the two encyclicals mentioned, has developed such a broad 'range of methods' that a new definition of the Catholic standpoint on them was desirable.

The new document indicates yet another reason for its composition: the growing gulf between exegesis and dogmatics. This was already noted in the 1989 document 'L'Interprétation des dogmes' from the International Theological Commission (published in *La Documentation Catholique* 89, 1990, 489–502). As insiders know, a line runs from this to the criticism of present-day Catholic exegesis of the Bible in the book *Schriftauslegung im Widerstreit. Zur Frage nach Grundlagen und Wert der Exegese heute* (Quaestiones Disputatae 117, Freiburg 1989), to which Cardinal Ratzinger has made a contribution and of which he is the editor. We should not dismiss this sweeping criticism ('expertocracy, a delight in hypotheses, historical positivism, a lack of theological vision and spirituality') because it comes from a particular theological camp. The gulf between dogmatics and exegesis is felt as a serious problem by professors and students in all theological faculties and seminaries of almost all Christian churches. Only with a more fundamentalist approach to either scripture or dogma does the problem disappear. Moreover it is good that the Papal Biblical Commission should have accepted this challenge, without making the question the comprehensive framework of the document.

It is impossible to provide a detailed survey of this new document in a column. A brief sketch of the four chapters must suffice. The first describes the present-day pluralism of exegetical methods. Each approach is described succinctly in essence, with none omitted. Of course the historical-critical method, linguistic and literary criticism are described, but also those methods which derive their means of working from modern humane sciences (sociology and cultural anthropology, psychology and psychoanalysis) or the problems of the present day (liberation theology and feminism). The second chapter discusses the hermeneutical problem of how one can avoid the fragmentation of exegesis with this great variety of methods. The attempt at integration is based on what present-day philosophy has to say about the interpretation of texts in a historical perspective. One's only wish is that this chapter had gone in more detail into the triangular relationship between author, text and reader. The third chapter discusses the characteristics of Catholic biblical interpretation. On the basis of 'methodological afterthought' one would expect that the document would take back what it had given earlier, but that is not the case. According to the document the unavoidable 'pre-understanding' of Catholic exegesis consists in the need to connect modern, scientific culture with the religious tradition which has it roots both in Israel and in the first Christian community. The last chapter indicates how exegesis can make use of insights for the faith community from the perspective of actualization, inculturation and church practice (liturgy, the pastorate and ecumenism).

One has to give this document a warm welcome. The following points are worth mentioning.

1. It is based on great expertise. The survey of the many contemporary exegetical methods is at the same time both penetrating and clear. Scholars can use it to test their own work with; teachers can use it with profit in their lessons. Probably the high quality of this part stems from the fact that the various paragraphs were handed over to specialists in each sphere. The document is thus a proof that the various international commissions which

are associated with the Roman dicasteria can play a unique role when they can bring together experts from all over the world to do their work in academic freedom, away from church politics and ideology.

2. The document does not stop at a description of present-day exegesis, but makes a substantial contribution to the worldwide discussion of how the different exegetical methods can converge in giving a meaning which avoids fragmentation. Above all the attempt to form a theory about the relationship between the historical and the literary approaches is valuable. In this respect the document breaks through the frontiers of the confessions and can have a stimulating effect on interdenominational biblical exegesis.

3. The document breathes an atmosphere of openness. While the practice of Catholic theology over recent decades has been deluged with restrictive documents from Rome in which the literary genres of warning and prohibition have been most dominant, this document is surprising in its attitude of endorsement and encouragement. The only thing that is really rejected is fundamentalist exegesis, because this in principle sees revelation in non-historical terms and as a result develops an ideology which is in conflict with the incarnation of the Word itself. Where there are further warnings, they tend to be more in relation to substance. In the passage on feminism the document is even unusually open for Roman attitudes: in a footnote there is an indication of the result of a vote in the commission. This relates to a warning against tendencies in feminism about 'power in the church'. The holding of a vote may be disappointing, but the fact that it is mentioned openly takes the sting out of the warning!

4. The document speaks clearly about the split between the trend which derives the meaning of a text from the history of its origin (diachrony) and the trend which thinks the final form of the text determinative (synchrony). The value of historical exegesis lies in the recognition of the historical character of God's word and its expression in the faith community. This bars the way to too easy a view of the contemporaneity of the present-day reader with the witness of the prophets and apostles, a view which is encouraged by a fundamentalist interpretation of e.g. biblical ethics and church order. Over against this the document also states explicitly that only the final form of the text is the expression of God's Word.

5. At a number of points one hears new voices: on the disparate independence of the Old Testament over against the New; the importance of Jewish biblical interpretation for the study of both Testaments; the significance of the history of the influence of the text and of the humane sciences; the danger of limiting the significance of scripture to what the

tradition has attached itself to instead of giving the Bible a critical function; the role of the local church in seeking the meaning of the Bible for itself; the poor as the privileged audience; the desirability of entrusting exegetical teaching in seminaries to women as well as to men; the need for the magisterium to listen to explanations that exegetes bring forward in freedom. This selection must suffice to illustrate the freshness of the document.

Is any more to be wished? Yes, certainly, the following. The authority of this declaration is defined by the status of the Papal Biblical Commission. 'This commission is not an organ of the magisterium but a working party of experts who speak in awareness of their responsibilities to scholarship and the church and know that they are supported in this by the confidence of the magisterium' (thus the accompanying letter). One need not be an expert in hermeneutics to be able to infer from this description that the magisterium can show its trust in the Papal Biblical Commission only by applying to itself the principles of the interpretation of scripture as the Commission has formulated it. That has not happened in many statements of the magisterium on the well-known major issues of church order and morality in recent decades. In them the argument from Holy Scripture has fallen well short of the norms of present-day exegesis. The Papal Biblical Commission document comes too late for the *Catechism of the Catholic Church* and for the encyclical *Veritatis Splendor*, but may we hope that we shall find its influence on future statements by the magisterium? At all events, this document reminds the magisterium and exegetes that their concerns should be coupled with the encouragement of the scriptures, that we might have hope (Romans 15.4).

Wim Beuken

The editors of the Special Column are Norbert Greinacher and Bas van Iersel. The content of the Special Column does not necessarily reflect the views of the Editorial Board of Concilium.

Contributors

SMAIL BALIĆ was born in Mostar in 1920, and after gaining his PhD in Vienna in 1945, began as a lecturer at the Superior School of Commerce there. From 1963 to 1983 he was expert adviser on oriental languages at the Austrian National Library and from 1983 to 1986 he worked with the Institute of Arabo-Islamic Sciences at the Goethe University in Frankfurt. He has been designated Professor of the Islamic Theological Faculty in Sarajevo. His most important publications are *Die Kultur der Bosniaken* (1973); *Ruf vom Minarett* (1984); *Das unbekannte Bosnien* (1992); *Der Islam im Spannungsfeld von Tradition und heutiger Zeit* (1993); *Der Islam europakonform*, 1994. He is co-editor of the *Lexikon religiöser Grundbegriffe*, ed. Adel T. Koury (1987), and was editor of the journal *Islam und der Westen* from 1980 to 1989.

Address: POB 11, 2261 Angern, Austria.

PATRICK D. GAFFNEY CSC teaches in the Department of Anthropology in the University of Notre Dame, Indiana, but is currently on leave teaching at the Queen of Apostles Philosophy Centre, Jinja, Uganda. He is a specialist in symbolic anthropology, religion and politics and Islamic societies, and has done extensive research in the Arab world, principally Egypt. He has published a number of articles in academic journals and his book *The Prophet's Pulpit: Islamic Preaching in Contemporary Egypt* will appear during 1994.

Address: University of Notre Dame, Department of Anthropology, Notre Dame, Indiana, USA.

RIFFAT HASSAN is a Muslim. She studied at an Anglican missionary school in Lahore, and was an undergraduate and graduate at the University of Durham, England, where she obtained her PhD on the work of Muhammad Iqbal. After working as Deputy Director of the Bureau of National Research and Reference for the Federal Government of Pakistan she moved to the USA in 1972 and has taught at

Villanova University, University of Pennsylvania, Oklahoma State University, Harvard Divinity School and the Iliff School of Theology. She has been Professor and Chairperson of the Religious Studies Programme at the University of Louisville, where she has taught since 1976, and has been intensively involved in developing feminist theology in Islam and participating in Jewish-Christian Muslim inter-religious dialogue. She has written numerous articles and her books include *The Sword and the Sceptre* (1977), *An Iqbal Primer* (1979), *The Bitter Harvest* (1977); she has also co-edited *Women's and Men's Liberation. Testimonies of the Spirit* (1991).

Address: University of Louisville, PO Box 17202, Louisville KY 40217 USA.

JUDO POERWOWIDAGDO was born in Java, Indonesia, in 1942 and studied theology at Jakarta Theological Seminary, San Francisco Theological Seminary and the University of Pittsburgh, where he gained his PhD. He has taught at the United Theological College and Faculty of Theology, Duta Wacana Christian University, and the University of Gadjah Mada, Indonesia, and is currently Executive Secretary in Ecumenical Theological Education on Unity and Renewal of the WCC in Geneva. He has written many articles on theology, education, communication and religion.

Address: World Council of Churches, 150 Route de Ferney, 1211 Geneva 20, Switzerland.

JOHN RENARD received a PhD in Islamic Studies from the Department of Near Eastern Languages and Civilizations in 1978, and since then has taught in the Faculty of Theological Studies, of Saint Louis University. He has had several dozen articles published in such journals as *The Muslim World, The Journal of the American Oriental Society, Hamdard Islamicus, The Journal of Ecumenical Studies* and the *Journal of Sophia Asian Studies*. He has written three books: *Ibn 'Abbād of Ronda: Letters on the Sufi Path* (1986), *In the Footsteps of Muhammad: Understanding the Islamic Experience* (1992), and *Islam and the Heroic Image: Themes in Literature and the Visual Arts* (1993).

Address: Saint Louis University, 3634 Lindell, St Louis, MO 63119, USA.

JOHN L. ESPOSITO is Professor of Religion and International Affairs and Director of the Center for Muslim-Christian Understanding: History and International Affairs at Georgetown University's School of Foreign Service, and Editor-in-Chief of Oxford University Press's *Encyclopedia of the Modern Islamic World*. Among his recent publications are: *The Islamic Threat: Myth or Reality?, Islam and Politics, Islam: The Straight Path* and *The Iranian Revolution: Its Global Impact*.

Address: Center for Muslim-Christian Understanding, Georgetown University, School of Foreigh Service, Washington D C 20057 – USA.

MOHAMMED ARKOUN was born in 1928 in Taourint Mimoun, Algeria. He studied in Oran, Algiers and Paris, where he gained his doctorate. He is now Professor of Islamology at the Universities of Paris III and VIII. His main publications are: *Contribution à l'étude de l'humanisme arabe au IVe/Xe siècle*, 1970; *Traité d'Ethique* (a French translation with introduction and notes of Miskawayh's *Tahdhîb al-Akhlâq*), 1969; *Essais sur la pensée islamique*, 1973; *La Pensée arabe*, 1975; *Comment lire le Coran?*, 1970.

Address: 44 Boulevard Magenta, 75010 Paris, France.

VINCENT J. CORNELL is Andrew Mellon Assistant Professor of Religion at Duke University, North Carolina. He gained his PhD in Islamic Studies at the University of California, Los Angeles with a prizewinning dissertation, *Mirrors of Prophethood: The Evolving Image of the Spiritual Master in the Western Maghrib from the Origins of Sufism to the End of the Sixteenth Century*, and has published a number of articles in international journals on Islamic thought, Islamic legal issues and the Islamic history of North Africa. A study of the doctrinal and poetic works of Abū Madyan is in preparation.

Address: Duke University, Box 90964, Durham, North Carolina, 27708–0964 USA.

ADOLFO GONZÁLEZ MONTES was born in Salamanca in 1946 and is a priest. He studied in Salamanca, Madrid, Tübingen and Rome, and has a degree in philosophy and literature and a doctorate in theology. He is Professor of Fundamental Theology at the Pontifical University of Salamanca, director of the Juan XXIII Ecumenical Centre in Salamanca, and editor of the journal *Diálogo Ecuménico*. Professor

González is also an adviser to the Spanish Episcopal Commission for Interconfessional relations, and to the Vatican's Pontifical Council for Unity. He is a member of the *Societas Oecumenica Europea* and has been for years a member of its executive. His most important publications include *Razón política de la fe cristiana*, Salamanca 1976; *Religión y nacionalismo. La doctrina luterana de los dos reinos como teología civil*, Salamanca 1982; and *Enchiridion oecumenicum*, Salamanca, Vol. 1, 1986; Vol. 2, 1993.

Address: Facultad de Teologia, Universidad Pontifica, Salamanca, Spain.

MAHMUD GAMAL-AD-DIN was born in 1930 and studied Islamic law in Cairo. From 1972 to 1980 he was a member of the Higher Committee of Islamic Legislation, first in Libya and then in the Egyptian People's Assembly; from 1984 to 1990 he was Vice-Prosecutor/Judge in the Egyptian Court and Counsellor and Vice-chairman of the Egyptian Court of Cassation. He is now Professor in the Judiciary Higher Institute in Riyadh, Saudi Arabia, and a member of the Islamic Research Synod, Al Azhar, Cairo. From 1980 to 1989 he was editor-in-chief of the journal *Manbar ul Islam*. His books include *Rights of the Woman in the Islamic Community*, 1981; *Islam and the Issue of Peace and War*, 1981; *The Contemporary Islamic State, ²1990; Contemporary Issues in the Islamic Call*, 1985; *Islam and Contemporary Political Problems,* and *Principles of Islamic Community*, ²1990; all in Arabic and published in Cairo.

Addresses: Al Imam Muhammad ibn Saud Islamic University, PB 5701, Riyadh, Kingdom of Saudi Arabia; · 11 Al-Khartoum Street, Al-Agouza-Giza, Cairo, Egypt.

HEINER BIELEFELDT was born in 1958 and studied philosophy and Catholic theology in Bonn and Tübingen. At present he is on a Humboldt grant at the University of Toronto. His publications include: *Neuzeitliches Freiheitsrecht und politische Gerechtigkeit. Perspektiven der Gesellschaftsvertragstheorien* (1990); *Zum Ethos der menschenrechtlichen Demokratie. Eine Einführung am Beispiel des Grundgesetzes* (1991), and with Johannes Schwartländer: *Christen und Muslime vor der Herausforderung der Menschenrechte* (1992); *Wiedergewinnung des Politischen. Eine Einführung in Hannah Arendts politischen Denken* (1993); *Kampf und Entscheidung. Politischer Existentialismus bei Carl Schmitt, Helmuth Plessner und Karl Jaspers* (1994).

Address: Juristische Fakultät der Universität Heidelberg, Friedrich-Ebert-Anlage 6–10, D–69117 Heidelberg, Germany.

ABDULAZIZ SACHEDINA was born in Lindi, Tanzania in 1942. He studied at Aligarh Muslim University, India, and Ferdorwsi University, Iran, before gaining his doctorate at the University of Toronto in 1976. Since then he has been Professor in the Department of Religious Studies at the University of Virginia. In addition to numerous articles he has written: *Islamic Messianism: The Idea of the Mahdi in Twelver Shi'ism*, 1980; *Human Rights and the Conflict of Cultures: Western and Islamic Perspectives on Religious Liberty*, 1988, and *The Just Ruler in Twelver Shi'ism: The Comprehensive Authority of the Jurist in Imamite Jurisprudence*, 1988.

Address: Department of Religious Studies, Cocke Hall, University of Virginia, Charlottesville, Virginia 22908, USA.

GERHARD BÖWERING was born in Germany; he studied philosophy in Würzburg and Munich, and then Islamic languages in Cairo and Lahore and theology in Montreal, where he gained his PhD at McGill University in 1975. Until 1984 he taught at the University of Pennsylvania in Philadelphia and since then has been Professor of Islamic Studies at Yale University, where he serves on the university council on Middle East Studies. He has been a visiting professor in Innsbruck and Princeton and received the award of the American Council of Learned Societies for the best first book in the history of religions for his monograph on Qur'anic hermeneutics.

Address: Department of Religious Studies, Yale University, PO Box 2160, New Haven, CT 06520, USA.

JANE DAMMEN MCAULIFFE is Chair of the Department for the Study of Religion at the University of Toronto and Director of its Center for the Study of Religion. Before that she was Associate Dean of the Candler School of Theology at Emory University in Atlanta, Georgia. Her recent works include *Qur'anic Christians: An Analysis of Classical and Modern Exegesis*, Cambridge 1991, and *Abassid Authority Affirmed: The Early Years of al Mansur*, New York 1993. She has been active in dialogue between Jews, Christians and Muslims and is consultant to the National Conference of Catholic Bishops as a member of the Muslim-Catholic dialogue in the United States.

Address: University of Toronto, Victoria College, 73, Queens' Park Crescent, Toronto, Ontario M5S 1K7, Canada.

HANS KÜNG was born in Sursee, near Lucerne, in 1928. From 1948 to 1955 he studied philosophy and theology at the Papal Gregorian Institute in Rome, and was ordained in 1954. In 1955 he studied at the Sorbonne and the Institut Catholique in Paris, and gained his doctorate in theology in 1957. After pastoral work at the Hofkirche in Luzern, in 1960 he was appointed Professor of Fundamental Theology in the University of Tübingen. Under Pope John XXIII he was appointed an official advisor to the Second Vatican Council. In 1963 he became Professor of Dogmatic and Ecumenical Theology and Director of the Institute for Ecumenical Research in Tübingen. Since 1980 he has held an independent chair as Professor for Ecumenical Theology as well as continuing as Director of the Institute for Ecumenical Research. His most recent publications are *Global Responsibility* (1990, ET 1991), *Judaism* (1991, ET 1992), *Mozart* (1991, ET 1992), *Credo* (1992, ET 1993), *A Global Ethic* (1993, with K.-J. Kuschel) and *Great Christian Thinkers* (1994). In 1993 his sixty-fifth birthday was celebrated with a *Festschrift*, *Hans Küng: Neue Horizonte des Glaubens und Denkens*, ed. K.-J. Kuschel and H. Häring, abbreviated ET *Hans Küng: New Horizons for Faith and Thought*.

Members of the Advisory Committee for Ecumenism

Directors

Hans Küng	Tübingen	Germany
Jürgen Moltmann	Tübingen	Germany

Members

Johannes Brosseder	Königswinter	Germany
Robert Clément SJ	Hazmieh	Lebanon
H. Czosnyka	St Louis	USA
André Dumas	Paris	France
John Erickson	Crestwood, NY	USA
Edward Farrington	Rome	Italy
David Ford	Cambridge	England
Bruno Forte	Naples	Italy
Alexandre Ganoczy	Würzburg	Germany
Adolfo González-Montes	Salamanca	Spain
Bernd Groth	Rome	Italy
Michael Hurley SJ	Belfast	Ireland
Zdenek Kucera	Prague	Czechoslovakia
Karl-Joseph Kuschel	Tübingen	Germany
Pinchas Lapide	Frankfurt/Main	Germany
Harry McSorley	Toronto, Ont.	Canada
Ronald Modras	St Louis, MO	USA
Ruth Page	Edinburgh	Scotland
Wolfhart Pannenberg	Grafelfing	Germany
Otto Pesch	Hamburg	Germany
Hermann Rüegger	Zurich	Switzerland
P. Samir Khalil	Paris	France
Alfonso Skowronek	Warsaw	Poland
Leonard Swidler	Philadelphia, PA	USA
Stephen Sykes	Ely	Great Britain
Lukas Vischer	Bern	Switzerland
Christos Yannaras	Athens	Greece

Concilium

Issues of *Concilium* to be published in 1994

1994/1: Violence against Women
Edited by Elisabeth Schüssler Fiorenza and M. Shawn Copeland

This issue aims not only to raise church consciousness about the existence of widespread violence against women but also to explore its significance for a feminist rearticulation of Christian theology. Accounts of women's experiences of violence are followed by discussions of cultural identity values, including the pornographic exploitation of women; a third part discusses the church's encouragement of violence against women and the issue ends with new means of feminine empowerment.

03024 2   February

1994/2: Christianity and Culture: A Mutual Enrichment
Edited by Norbert Greinacher and Norbert Mette

This issue explores that point in the relationship between Christianity and cultures where a culture discloses new dimensions of the gospel as well as being the object of criticism in the light of the gospel, a process known as 'inculturation'. Part One examines fundamental aspects of inculturation, Part Two looks at test cases (in Coptic Christianity, Zaire, Pakistan, Latin America and Canada) and Part Three reflects thinking on inculturation.

03025 0   April

1994/3   Islam: A Challenge for Christianity
Edited by Hans Küng and Jürgen Moltmann

The first section describes experiences of Islam in Africa, Central Asia, Indonesia, Pakistan and Europe and the second the threat felt by Christians from Islam and by Muslims from Christianity. The final section explores the challenges posed by Islam; monotheism, the unity of religion and politics, Islamic views of human rights and the position Islam occupies as a religion coming into being after Christianity and Judaism.

03026 9   June

1994/4: Mysticism and the Institutional Crisis

Edited by Christian Duquoc and Gustavo Gutiérrez

The decline in mainstream church membership suggests that a less institutional and more mystical approach to religion is called for, and that this is an approach which the churches should encourage. This issue looks at mystical movements in various parts of the globe, from Latin America through Africa to Asia, and asks how they can become less marginalized than they have been in the past.

03022 7   August

1994/5: Catholic Identity

Edited by James Provost and Knut Walf

How is an institution, a movement, a social teaching, or even an individual 'Catholic' today? The question has many applications, in terms of identity, discipline, teaching and so on. This issue explores its ramifications with relation to particular theological and canonical issues.

03028 5   October

1994/6: Why Theology?

Edited by Werner Jeanrond and Claude Jeffré

This issue surveys the programme, methods and audience for theology today, at a time when its status as an academic discipline is no longer possible, and in many contexts it cannot be engaged in without interference from state and church authorities.

03029 3   December

Concilium Subscription Information - outside North America

Individual Annual Subscription (six issues): £30.00

Institution Annual Subscription (six issues): £40.00

Airmail subscriptions: add £10.00

Individual issues: £8.95 each

New subscribers please return this form:
for a two-year subscription, double the appropriate rate

(for individuals)   £30.00   (1/2 years)   . . . .

(for institutions)   £40.00   (1/2 years)   . . . .

Airmail postage
outside Europe +£10.00   (1/2 years)   . . . .

                                        Total . . . .

I wish to subscribe for one/two years as an individual/institution
(delete as appropriate)

Name/Institution . . . .

Address . . . .

. . . .

. . . .

I enclose a cheque for . . . . payable to SCM Press Ltd

Please charge my Access/Visa/Mastercard no. . . . .

Signature . . . . .Expiry Date . . . .

Please return this form to:
SCM PRESS LTD 26-30 Tottenham Road, London N1 4BZ

CONCILIUM

The Theological Journal of the 1990s

Now available from Orbis Books

Founded in 1965 and published six times a year, *Concilium* is a world-wide journal of theology. Its editors and essayists encompass a veritable 'who's who' of theological scholars. Not only the greatest names in Catholic theology, but exciting new voices from every part of the world, have written for this unique journal.

Concilium exists to promote theological discussion in the spirit of Vatican II, out of which it was born. It is a catholic journal in the widest sense: rooted firmly in the Catholic heritage, open to other Christian traditions and the world's faiths. Each issue of *Concilium* focusses on a theme of crucial importance and the widest possible concern for our time. With contributions from Asia, Africa, North and South America, and Europe, *Concilium* truly reflects the multiple facets of the world church.

Now available from Orbis Books, *Concilium* will continue to focus theological debate and to challenge scholars and students alike.